I'M NOT A LEADER

Release the leader within you

Mark Herbert

I'M ~~NOT~~ A LEADER

Release the leader within you

Mark Herbert

I love the premise of this book. Many of the world's most remarkable leaders, from Moses to Malala, were reluctant and even insecure at first. This is a time when families, communities, businesses and nations need leadership as never before, and this book will help us all to step up to the plate and make a real difference.

—Pete Greig,
Best-selling author, Ambassador to Tearfund,
Founder of 24/7Prayer International,
Senior Pastor of Emmaus Road Church

Mark brings a perceptive view on what it takes to be a leader. His ability to articulate information, challenge thinking with care, and share anecdotes and examples with clarity make this book a must-read. His heart-centred approach to leadership is what our new age is calling for. This book captures the essence of leading for our future.

—Mary-Anne Murphy,
Author, Speaker, Coach

The world has never been this volatile and unpredictable. Planning for the future is increasingly becoming a very difficult affair. The world now demands a new breed of leader - an astute leader who can extrapolate from 'what is' and translate it into 'what could be.' Only a leader of note is capable of this feat. This highly recommended book will help you become the sort of leader the world yearns for. From the first chapter to the last, you will be amazed at the leadership insights the book contains.

—Hon. Neal Rijkenberg,
Government Minister of Finance,
Kingdom of Eswatini

I have known Mark since he was 13 years old and seen him consistently grow in character and stature. His courage and determination are obvious, as is his desire to serve others. Thinking and writing for those who don't see themselves as leaders is an example of these qualities. This book is full of practical ideas which will benefit anyone who reads and we, at C-me, recommend this book to you wholeheartedly.

—Simon Wilsher,
Founder of C-me Colour Profiling

As a mother, doctor and small business owner, Mark's book has helped me understand how to lead with humility and gentleness in work and home environments, places that are constantly changing and throwing up new challenges. His personable style of writing and applicable ideas made this a great read after a busy day and help me apply those same ideas the next morning.

—Helen Eckley,
Palliative Care Doctor,
Small Business Owner and Mother of Three

At the heart of leadership is service and, having known Mark since his undergraduate days, I can testify with confidence that he exemplifies servant-hearted leadership. This book is, therefore, authentic as well as insightful. Enjoy it!

—Graham Daniels,
Director of Cambridge United Football Club
and National Director of Christians in Sport

"I'm ~~not~~ a leader" is simply brilliant. The short, punchy chapters with lots of real-life examples, make it accessible to everyone. After several years of school headship, reading the book has helped me to pause and reflect on my own leadership. The insightful 'nudges' at

the end of each chapter particularly help me with this. The material and structure make this book a great resource to use when coaching and developing leaders. I would highly recommend getting yourself a copy.

— **Verity Lambert-Dale,**
Headteacher, Purley Way Primary School, Croydon

If you are just starting out on your leadership journey or aren't sure whether you really want to take on that first leadership role you've been offered, this book is for you. Full of practical, down to earth wisdom and great reflection exercises, it will help you establish a strong foundation so that you can lead in a way that is unique to who you are, yet centred on what is best for those you lead.

— **Andy Matheson,**
Former Oasis International Director (2001-14),
Leadership Trainer and Coach with Moringa

This book is a treasure trove of tools for those aspiring to lead their private and public organizations to success. Leadership practitioners will do well to sharpen their skills through this book. The author's unique style of expression effortlessly lures the reader into self-inspection which is necessary for any leader to grow to the next level. It is a must-read for leaders in the demanding world of commerce, as well as non-profits.

— **E. Nathi Dlamini,**
CEO Business Eswatini (Chamber of Commerce)

Book commendations are normally given by well-known professionals and those with letters after their name. I'm just an ordinary 20-year old guy, so the fact that Mark has asked me to commend this book tells you a lot about him as a leader. He has mentored me for a while now and has always emphasised that leadership is not about position, but rather about influence. The book speaks of the importance of fostering humility and maintaining an attitude of continual learning. As Mark coaches me, I see each leadership skill mentioned in this book being practised by him. I always get the sense that we are journeying together and I'm encouraged to know that leadership isn't an unattainable goal but an achievable, ongoing practice. It is clear that the wonderful help this book brings has come straight from his heart. Don't miss out!

—**Josh Soal,**
Author's mentee and friend

I'M ~~NOT~~ A LEADER

Release the leader within you

Mark Herbert

First Edition
March 2021

Diagrams and images produced by Chris and Anna Evans at Sherry Design
www.sherrydesign.co.uk

ACKNOWLEDGEMENTS

There are many people I would like to thank, who have influenced the writing of this book.

Thank you to the countless people who have set an example to me throughout my life. Many of you would probably not consider yourself to be leaders but you have inspired me in different ways, often without even knowing it.

Thank you, Michelle (*michelleemerson.co.uk*), for your invaluable help with publication and Pete Beckett (*petebeckett.com*) for producing my website (*leader-full.co.uk*). Thank you, Chris and Anna (*sherrydesign.co.uk*) for designing the book cover and producing the internal artwork.

Thank you, Graham and Juliet (Mum and Dad!), for the huge personal sacrifices you made to enable me to have such a happy and fulfilled childhood. My education at *Monkton* was where the seeds for much of my own leadership were sown.

Thank you to the *Rank Foundation* for the leadership scholarship you awarded me in 2001. This vote of confidence twenty years ago inspired me to work at being a more effective leader and commit to developing young leaders today.

Thank you, Ray, David, Emma, Rosie, Richard, Guy, Al, Sue, Jane, John, Simon, Pete, Mark, Kathy and Robbie, for your constant source of encouragement. You have all been great friends as well as mentors to me. Thank you for never giving up on me, even when I have made mistakes. You have taught me the importance of leading myself well – a journey I am still very much on. Particular thanks to you, Kathy, for your meticulous help with proof reading. You certainly made up for my failure to listen in grammar lessons at school!

Thank you, Steph, for giving honest feedback when my first draft was a little clunky. This sort of feedback can only really come from one's wife! Thank you too for your patience and encouragement which has kept me going, especially when I've had to work late into the evenings to get the manuscript finished.

Most of all, thank you, John, for being my best and most consistent friend. Thank you for the great example you are to me of someone who never gives up seeking to lead himself well. Thanks too for always encouraging me to do the same. This book is dedicated to you.

CONTENTS

FOREWORD

*Leadership is not always instinctive. It can be taught
... but is it always learnt?*

It would indeed be bizarre if, given my professional duties as a Professor of Leadership and teaching weekly, I did not reflect continuously, not just on the well-rehearsed theories of leadership that abound in so many books, videos, podcasts and articles... but also on what I have observed in my near 45 years of business and public life. My conundrum is this: we say leadership can be taught and, of course, if it couldn't what would be the point of a book like this? But *is teaching leadership the same as learning leadership, imbibing, embracing and practising leadership*? How come, I ask, evidently great public leaders are often followed by hapless, corrupt and diminutive figures, whose poverty of principles push back the progress made by their strong value-based predecessors? How come, I ask, is there so often a massive gulf between the *idealism* that leadership-thinking pursues and the *practices* of those who claim to have got it .....but evidently haven't!!

When we look for icons in living memory, we have sight of no better an example than Nelson Mandela. Once a prisoner, then a President. He was smart and astoundingly humble. I met him twice in London and I could sense and then see the aura of settled contentment and the uninhibited delight of sparking a national transformation that was the wonder of the world. I love this insightful reflection from him: '*Lead from the back – and let others believe they are in front.*' How many in Presidential positions would ever contemplate that?! But he did. And, with strategic intent and forceful deliberation, he won his way in law and won the world's adoration, putting a riven nation on a pathway to healing. But those who followed him in office were and are to this day hopelessly inadequate as leaders and embarrassingly visionless. This represents an all too common tragedy of today: that great leaders and golden moments in leadership become quickly tarnished, exposing a dimness of reception and the failure to imbibe exceptional leadership modelling. This reveals the gap on which I am musing.

It was Bertrand Russell, the great 19th century philosopher and historian, who had observed this very phenomenon, commenting that '*The whole problem with the world is that fools and fanatics are always so certain of themselves, but wiser people are so full of doubts.*' Why is this? Why is it that irrational radicals and angry mobs are confident, and the highly intelligent and perspective-seeking minority are so timid? And why, with democracies, it is all too easy to push extremists to office, not because of their great merit but because of their great rhetoric, volume or imagery? And this then gets confused with leadership!

Surely we need to get to a place where there is *evidence* of someone acting like and looking like and thinking like a leader should? Only then should they be credited with either the title or the office or the opportunity. This might mean that those we expect to lead, don't, and we all end up better for it. Perhaps it is the unlikely leader who might then have opportunity to step up and flourish?

We all need to reflect on the fact that it wasn't an accident that Europe faced a vile war in the 1930s and 40s, driven by an elected cultured academic whose rhetorical leadership led his people astray. Pulled away from their great history of arts and culture and philosophy and learning, and the wisdom of centuries gone before, a nation then turned towards devastation and mass murder. Unforgettable public compliance rated their leader way over and above the legacy of a nation's public purpose. And even as I write this, the great example of Germany's Angela Merkel, as she draws to an end 16 years of effective leadership from behind, is not being followed in her party as the ideal example for great statesmanship and the country is being tempted again by radicalism and not reason. Why doesn't good leadership transfer?

Maybe the answer lies in accepting that, although leadership - well, good, efficacious, purposeful, servant-orientated leadership - can be taught, it doesn't necessarily follow that it will be embraced and so there remains a great problem.

Unless men and women, younger and older, start their leadership journey based on a foundation of secure principles and values, it's likely, most likely, that they will know the philosophy but not the practice. This leads me to reflect further that what is less needed is relentless rhetoric around leadership, and instead more vigorous *application* through perpetual active service.

I saw this in practice some years ago. A highly effective and successful Chief Executive of a major global retail and investment bank was weary of talking to his board about the values he felt should guide their decision-making. So, instead of lectures on leadership or commending even more books, he took the board for a working retreat in a destitute community in Eastern Africa where they had to do the hard work that so many men and women face day in, day out – building toilets and water systems, shoring up shoddy school buildings and dealing with diseased and fearful children – and then come together around a table and try to make dispassionate decisions about interest rates or lending policy. It changed everything. They had gone from the ideals to the pragmatics, and it was the foundation principles of the bank's approach to fairness and dignity that truly won out over the immediacy of more profit. People came to matter more, and decisions were different as a result.

I'm ~~not~~ a Leader is a smart title for a book. It is a much needed invitation for some to step into leadership for the first time when it would be all too easy for them to assume that this is someone else's responsibility. The book is also an invitation to us all to consider what we mean by leadership. We need to learn how to learn, then learn to be better leaders and then, most importantly, put this into practice.

I have concluded that we learn leadership through truth heard, read, understood, embraced, imbibed, practised, modelled, affirmed, confirmed and instilled. Then it becomes instinctive. And then no one can say '*I am NOT a leader*', because we can all serve … and so learn … and thus learn to be leaders. May it be so.

Lord Dr Michael Hastings of Scarisbrick, CBE
Chancellor of Regent's University London,
Professor of Leadership at the Stephen R Covey Leadership
Center, Huntman Business School, Chair of the London
Chamber of Commerce and Industry Black Business Association
Vice President, UNICEF; Chair, Council of ZANE (Zimbabwe)
Co-Founder, My Brother's Keeper – a positive
prisoner development process

March 2021

A NOTE FROM THE AUTHOR

A look across the years reveals that I have always been fascinated by leadership.

1991 – My first outing to the Bath rugby ground to watch our local side play. I loved watching the players huddle up before kick-off, with the captain standing in the middle of the circle motivating his players. I always wondered what was being said and aspired to be a leader like that.

1995 – This was my first time in an aeroplane, and I was fascinated by the pilot in his smart uniform and the professionalism he displayed. I can still remember when he allowed me to stand in the entrance to his cockpit and gave me a tour of all the flashing lights and controls and then turned to the co-pilot to provide instructions for our descent. He led with such assured authority.

1998 – The first time I led a sports team out onto the pitch and the sense of responsibility that came with this. We lost, but I was asked to captain the side again the next week. I was only a teenager but was already learning that leadership was not always about winning.

2006 – Read Dame Ellen MacArthur's account of breaking the world record for sailing solo around the world. Her determination and resilience made such an impression on me. She was an inspirational example to me of impressive self-leadership.

2007 – A terrible sporting injury. This event, and many more minor ones before, taught me patience and challenged my sense of identity. Who was I when I was unable to be active? How could I still have influence from the side-lines? I was learning that leadership influence can come from any place. Attitude is far more important than position.

2010 – Sadly watched a friend die of motor neurone disease. I was amazed at his positivity and insistence on asking after other people, even though he was suffering so much himself. I was learning about selflessness – a crucial skill of leadership.

I have worked alongside and witnessed some amazing leaders – men and women who have taught me through their approach and attitude as much as their actions. Many of them have come from cultures different from my own which has helped broaden my perspectives. I have also witnessed some poor leadership. At the time it frustrated me, but I have since tried to learn from these experiences.

I have been an effective leader on many occasions and am thankful for the encouragements I have received along the way. I have also messed up horribly and let people down.

Every one of these experiences (and countless others that I cannot mention here) have shaped the leader I am today. The essence of leadership is about positively influencing others through relationships. My aim is to continue growing as this kind of leader each day. I hope this book will play a part in helping you to do the same.

I was asked recently by a younger man what the most important things might be for him to focus on as a leader. These were the seven I suggested to him:

1. **Cultivate a growth mindset.**

   Many people will be quick to offer you advice in life. Whilst there may be great value in this, let life-experiences be your greatest mentor. Always look for the learning in every situation, read widely, ask questions and listen carefully. There is always more to learn.

2. **Guard your heart.**

   Leading yourself well and fostering healthy attitudes is crucial if you are to flourish under pressure. How you respond to pressure says a great deal about you as a person and as a leader. Many of our attitudes are driven by the desires of our heart. Having a healthy heart will therefore feed healthy leadership. Put simply, healthy things grow.

3. **Resist the urge to control.**

   Control can take many forms and is often so subtle that we don't realise we are becoming a controlling leader. It is important to ask ourselves each day how we can empower others to flourish. Equally important is to resist the feeling that we need to have an opinion on everything or be involved in every decision.

4. **Listen more than you speak.**

   Few leaders do.

5. **Get on and lead.**

   Don't wait to be given a title or formal recognition that you are a leader before you start leading.

Leading is about having a positive influence on others - you can start that today. Whenever I have been in a role that requires the appointment of a new leader, I always look for the people who are already leading. They are most often the kind of people who are *just getting on with it* without drawing attention to themselves.

6. **Take responsibility for the next generation.**

However old you are, always be on the lookout for a leader with less experience. Seek to be a positive influence in their life. Leadership doesn't start when we are adults. Sadly too much leadership training does.

7. **Serve.**

Our aim in leadership ought always to be founded on a desire to see others flourish. We can achieve far more together than we ever can alone. Effective leaders care about people. As soon as leadership becomes about us, we stop leading. Are you a leader worth imitating?

Which of the above might be most helpful for you to focus on?

Here's to your ongoing leadership development and mine.

Mark Herbert

April 2021

Want to connect?
www.leader-full.co.uk
mark@leader-full.co.uk

IMAGINE

Imagine a world full of leaders. Extra-ordinary leaders with a clear and compelling vision and the ability to inspire others with this vision. Leaders who are able to communicate clearly and persuasively, rooting this in shared values. Imagine a world of leaders who are truly full of leadership, rather than being full of themselves. Imagine a world where leaders choose to serve. Imagine the impact!

Where can these sorts of leaders be found – the leaders the world needs most? We might naturally look to the high flyers from school or the people with the most impressive CVs or business portfolios. Many such people are great leaders - but not always. Maybe the answer is to look closer to home. Perhaps you are one of them. Yes, *you*.

I'm ~~not~~ a leader has been written to challenge anyone who does not think they are a leader or ever could be one. It's been written to challenge you by asserting that the statement *"I'm not a leader"* isn't necessarily true. Numerous leadership opportunities exist in our world, lying unfulfilled and waiting for someone to step into them; someone just like you. What is holding you back?

> *'I'm not qualified.'*
> *'I'm not old enough.'*

'I'm not ready.'
'I've never been recognised before.'
'I'm not very confident.'
'Others around me are better.'
'I've messed up too many times.'
'I'm just not a leader.'

These are all legitimate things to *feel* but this negative self-talk may end up suppressing significant opportunity for you to grow personally as well as make a huge positive difference in the lives of others.

Leadership is a choice, first of all to take responsibility in leading ourselves well - ensuring we remain emotionally healthy, humble and hungry in order that we keep on growing. Leadership also requires the choice to commit to investing in relationships. Understanding people will help us positively influence them and this is what leadership is all about.

Having worked in education, charity and the corporate worlds, close to home as well as overseas, I have been fortunate to have been impacted by a range of leaders operating in very different contexts. The single biggest thing they have taught me is the importance of relationships as THE key to positively influencing people. The choice we all have to make is whether or not we will commit to entering into life-giving relationships with others.

Leadership is not a destination to be reached or a badge of honour to be worn. It is not a skill to be learned on a course (even though courses can be helpful). Instead, leadership is fundamentally an attitude of commitment to personal and collective transformation. Growing as a leader involves going on a journey; a journey that will be different for every person. The journey may not be straightforward and it may at times end up costing you – leadership is seldom easy. Yet embarking on the adventure that is leadership is so often the choice that leads to greatest satisfaction.

If you have come to this book doubting that you could ever be a leader, *I'm ~~not~~ a leader* is for you. I hope you finish the book inspired that the leader within you *can* be released and that you will discover the unique contribution that *you* can make.

Imagine the impact *you* could have!

INTRODUCTION

As the Covid-19 pandemic rolls on, the whole world has been asking when we will get back to normal. Conceding that this is unlikely (maybe impossible?), talk has turned to establishing a *'new normal'*. Perhaps we ought to go one step further. Could we be entering a future where there will be *'no normal'*?

Our world is complex, volatile and uncertain. A constantly changing world requires us to be constantly learning, unlearning and indeed re-learning. Most people are more globally connected than ever before, and the need for genuine global citizenship has never been greater. We simply cannot afford to ignore this. Responsibility and accountability lie at the heart of our obligations towards one another.

In many areas of society, we are creating problems for ourselves and others faster than we are overcoming them. Perhaps the most pronounced of these relate to environmental stewardship, increasing disparity between rich and poor, and social pandemics such as isolation, loneliness and a crisis of personal identity. Each of these problems bears witness to the undeniable fact that our world needs better leaders. Those who think they could never be a leader need to be encouraged to step up to the challenge.

With this in mind, *I'm not a leader* focuses on six key areas of leadership development. There is a natural progression to the six Parts of the book, but it has also been written in such a way that each chapter can stand alone. This gives you the option of working through it sequentially (perhaps as part of your personal development or as training material to deliver to others), or simply picking out the chapters that immediately appeal to you. I'd certainly encourage you to return to the book regularly and use it as an ongoing resource.

We begin in **Parts 1 and 2** by reflecting on ourselves. What does it mean and what will it look like to know and lead ourselves well? In many ways this is foundational to leadership yet remains something that is easy to overlook. A key area of focus is reflecting on the people we are becoming. None of us is the finished article and none of our backgrounds is so broken that it is irredeemable. We each have a unique story and this story shapes both who we are today and who we are becoming. It is crucial that we come to understand this so that we lead out of who we are, rather than some external expectation of who we ought to be.

Part 3 is aimed at helping us understand others. Leadership is deeply relational so, if we are to be effective leaders, we need to become adept at deeply understanding other people. We will consider issues such as vulnerability and authenticity as well as reflect on what it means to truly appreciate and learn from others, even those we find most challenging.

In **Parts 4 and 5** we will begin to bring together and apply Parts 1 to 3, thinking about what it takes to communicate effectively. We will consider the role of listening, adapting behaviours and sharing stories as powerful means of communication. We will then look at communication in the context of conflict. These chapters deliberately touch on issues we may naturally wish to ignore. But if we engage each of these issues with a healthy attitude, we can grow significantly.

Part 6 addresses what it will look like to help others lead. The focus here is on multiplying leadership and creating healthy cultures of learning and trust in order to support the flourishing of others.

Each of the forty-eight chapters in this book is deliberately short. This is partly in recognition of busy leaders who often feel stretched and time-poor. The short chapters are also a response to my own frustration of many good books on leadership saying in one hundred words what could easily be said in ten.

You may notice that few of the chapters contain many stories or personal anecdotes. Again, this is deliberate. In many ways the purpose of this book is to act as a stimulus for you to attach your own stories and apply the principles to your own context. The aim of the book is to act as a conversation starter, asking searching questions and then creating space for reflection. To aid this, each chapter ends with a few suggested 'nudges' designed to prompt further thinking and group discussion.

I'm ~~not~~ a leader has been written in a style and format that is accessible to young and old, experienced and novice. It is principally designed for those of you who think you are not a leader, to inspire you to release the leader within you. Leadership is a journey which we can all walk together, learning from one another at each stage. My hope is that what you read here will bring greater depth and insight to your character and skills, that you might have a positive influence on those around you.

For more information, please visit **www.leader-full.co.uk**

PART 1

KNOWING YOURSELF

"Know thyself"

Inscription at the Temple of Apollo,
Delphi in Greece (Fourth Century AD)

We cannot lead others until we first lead ourselves. This presupposes that we know ourselves. What makes *you* uniquely you? Each person has an individual story to tell. Your story influences who you are and is shaping the person you are becoming. Knowing yourself frees you to lead out of who you are, rather than out of a felt need to fulfil a stereotype or another person's expectations. How well do you know yourself?

CHAPTER 1

SLOW DOWN – GIVE YOURSELF SPACE TO THINK

We live in an incredibly fast-paced world that runs on a mixture of adrenalin and technology. The former drives us to do more and the latter enables it. It's the perfect team! The flip side to all this is that we are often left leading a frantic life, overcommitted and regularly on the brink of burnt out. This is just as much an existential problem as it is a health one. Our busyness leaves us with little or no time to think and our identity ends up being driven by what we do, instead of who we are. (We will return to this in Chapter 5.)

As you reflect on these opening thoughts, I'd encourage you to pause and try to answer these two questions:

1. Who am I when I am not doing anything?
2. Is the pace of what I am doing damaging the person I am becoming?

Growing up I loved being a part of the Army Cadets. Each year we would participate in a march-and-shoot competition in the sand dunes of Penhale, Cornwall. This involved a five-mile run, carrying our rifles and loaded bergens, followed by a shooting challenge under timed pressure. The competition was assessed on both the run time and the shooting accuracy. In an eagerness to get to the shoot as quickly as possible, it was always tempting to sprint the final part of the run in an attempt to gain some time on fellow competitors. Instead, our team always walked the last fifty metres. Whilst it slowed down our run time slightly, the strategy enabled us to get to the range less out of breath and more ready to shoot accurately. It turned out it was the shooting accuracy and not the run time that differentiated the winners from second place.

Applying this analogy to leadership, do we ever intentionally slow down the work we are doing (the run) in order to think more clearly (the shoot)? Busyness is perhaps the biggest enemy to clear thinking. We need to learn to *think* about our thinking.

So, what can we do to overcome these issues? Here are two suggestions: *White Space* and the *1:59 Principle*.

White Space

White Space is time intentionally set aside for resting or thinking. For those of us who are busy people, our diaries inevitably become filled up with tasks to complete unless we intentionally set aside time that is protected from tasks. Try setting regular calendar appointments and simply call them *white space*. An appointment is made that is not allowed to be removed or invaded by something else. Creating *white space* will mean saying 'no' to some things, but remember that every 'no' is a 'yes' to something else. Why not give it a go?

This discipline is a great way of regularly recalibrating the pace at which you are working and can help create a more sustainable cadence to life's rhythms.

My own habit is to build in a twenty-minute period of *white space* on a daily basis, a two-hour period every week and a full day every three months. What might work well for you? There will always be potential excuses of why there is simply no time for *white space*. Perhaps this is all the more reason to fight for it with persistent intentionality.

The 1:59 Principle

The *1:59 Principle* is based on the conviction that one minute of clear and deliberate thinking can transform the next fifty-nine minutes of activity. We can all be guilty of ploughing into the next task, desiring to use every minute efficiently. How might pausing for the first minute help sharpen your mindset, help distil the key question that needs addressing and enable you to remain focussed? A one-minute pause is tiny, relative to the huge benefit it can bring to all that follows. Thinking first and then acting brings very different outcomes from acting first and thinking later. Try to find something memorable that can act as a reminder in the moment. It could be as simple as setting regular reminders or alarms on your phone, until the habit becomes more habitual.

The most effective leaders know when to push hard and when to slow down, using the slower time to think. How are you getting on?

Nudges

✎ Where in a typical week could you intentionally create space to slow down and put into practice the *white space* and *1:59* principles?

✎ In what ways is the pace at which you live your life having an impact on the person you are becoming?

✎ What daily habit could you commit to that will help you relax? What will you do to ensure this habit becomes a non-negotiable priority?

CHAPTER 2

LOOK BACK – REFLECT ON WHERE YOU HAVE COME FROM

We cannot understand ourselves if we do not understand where we have come from. History matters because what has passed has much to teach us. Where are the *places* that carry most meaning for you? Who are the *people* who have had the most significant impact on you? What are the *patterns* of behaviour they have taught you? These places, people and patterns will have shaped your story in a unique way. It is *your* story - the story that explains, at least in part, the person you are today.

As you reflect on your story, how do you feel? What are you most proud of? What do you regret? Some of us have backgrounds we look back on with fondness. Others of us have backgrounds we would rather forget. The key in both is to learn to use where we have come from to propel us positively into the future.

An essential part of your self-understanding as a leader is to recognise that who you are may have been *shaped* by your background, but this does not need to *define* who you are. Your background neither need define you nor hold you back. No matter how humble your background, there is no reason why your future cannot be extraordinary. Similarly, you ought not to feel constrained by your background, as if certain paths are somehow off-limits because they break from generational patterns. What you do is never as important as the sort of person you are becoming. Being a leader who has a secure identity founded on who you *are*, as opposed to what you *do*, is vital to being effective.

Here are three examples of people with differing backstories. As you reflect on each, try not to get distracted by any potential challenges these backgrounds present. Instead, look for the opportunities. How does each person's story have the potential to help shape them positively as a leader?

Meet Lucy. She was one of four siblings. They grew up in a middle-class home, enjoyed nice holidays and attended the best local schools. Outwardly she had it all together. She looked like the epitome of a high-flying success story. Sadly, however, inside she was breaking. Her childhood had been about keeping up a particular façade. Everyone around her looked to her family as the 'perfect model' - whatever that is! The reality was very different. Her parents' marriage was at crisis point: her mum drank heavily, and her dad was rarely present. There was little joy in the home. Life to Lucy's family was all about giving an impression of confidence and success. Below the surface, so much was in fact fragile.

Meet Tommy. He was an only child and grew up in foster care. His mother had died soon after his birth and his Dad walked out on him, unable to cope with the responsibility. Tommy lived with five different foster families before he was old enough to apply for council-run accommodation of his own. Stability and continuity were not things he had ever experienced. Despite this, he passed all his school exams and went on to apply for an apprenticeship in furniture making.

Meet Kate. She had a stable childhood and went on to get a master's degree in engineering from Cambridge. She spent the next ten years working for the same software development company, based in the Netherlands. Kate always had positive appraisals, was likeable and hard-working. Frustratingly, however, she never got chosen for promotion. Her colleagues were driven and far pushier, rising up the career ladder quickly. It seemed like Kate had been forgotten.

Reflecting on these stories (and indeed the backstory of anyone you meet) could prove to be a great exercise in learning to spot the future potential that lies hidden in others. In turn this will also help you become better at interpreting your own story in positive ways.

Remember the questions we began with? Where are the *places* that carry most meaning for you? Who are the *people* who have had the most significant impact on you? What are the *patterns* of behaviour they have taught you? As you look over your shoulder to the past, it is these places, people and patterns that are integral to your story. How could you use each one as a positive springboard into the future?

Nudges

- Spend some time reflecting on your story – the highs and lows, the successes and failures. What are you most proud of? What do you most regret?

- As you reflect on patterns of behaviour developed in your childhood, which behaviours are most life-giving? Which are most life-depleting?

- In what ways could your background (whether positive or negative) be used positively to propel you into the future?

CHAPTER 3

LOOK AROUND - THINK ABOUT WHERE YOU ARE TODAY

Having looked back and reflected on where you have come from and the things that make your story unique, you would also be wise to look around at your present. But beware of two dangers: either wanting to live in the past or wanting to live in the future. Whilst the past can shape today and be used as a springboard into the future, each day we wake with a choice: what we will do *now*. Understanding your present reality is vital to understanding yourself clearly.

As you rest in your present reality, take a moment first to express gratitude for all the people who have helped you get to this point. Then look around and consider the following questions: Where are you at today? How does this feel? Is it the place you want to be? Is it the place you expected to be? How are you spending your time each day? What is the state of your heart? How would you assess your character? It might be helpful to ask other people to feed into this process. Their honesty could be a great gift to you. What is their assessment of the person you are today? How effective do they feel you are as a leader?

Here are four perspectives to be aware of as you go through the above process: be honest, be open, be ready, be you.

Be honest with what you see. Try to celebrate the positives without deflection and face up to the inconvenient facts without excuses. So much of the art of leadership is being honest with yourself about yourself – not thinking of yourself more highly than you ought, but also not thinking of yourself more lowly than you ought.

Be open to what others share. If you respect them deeply enough, you will be willing for them to lead you to a place of discomfort at times. Equally, allow yourself to be encouraged by their encouragement. (We will think more about the role of Challengers and Cheerleaders in Chapter 14.)

Be ready to change. The whole point of self-reflection is for it to propel us forwards with more energy, focus, freedom and purpose. People change which means leaders must learn to become more comfortable with change as well.

Be you. A potentially destructive force always exists with self-reflection. It is the power of comparison. People-pleasing is exhausting and will inhibit your leadership. No two leaders are the same because no two people are the same. Leading with authenticity is about leading out of who we are. What makes *you* uniquely you? What are the specific gifts you have that can contribute positively today to the lives of those around you?

A crucial element of knowing ourselves is being honest about the place we are currently in. This helps us as leaders to play to our strengths and be open to ongoing development in weaker areas. Are you currently being honest with what you see, and with what others point out in you?

Nudges

- What do you think is your greatest strength and who has been the most positive influence on its formation in you?

- Try to identify a character trait, an attitude or a behaviour that you recognise is life-depleting for you and which you want to seek help in changing.

- Ask a trusted friend to share with you what they perceive to be your greatest strength and your biggest area for development.

CHAPTER 4

LOOK FORWARD – TAKE HOPE FROM WHO YOU ARE BECOMING

Whilst it is important to understand the people we are today, the people we are becoming matters even more. Life is never static and every new experience we go through can be used positively for our growth in order to equip us for the next moment.

The second century Greek philosopher, Epictetus, once stated, *"This is our predicament. Over and over again, we lose sight of what is important and what isn't."*[1] I would argue that the people we are becoming is probably the most important thing about us. Our lives carry a particular dignity when we recognise our infinite worth whilst at the same time seeing that we are works in progress.

---

[1] Epictetus, *The Art of Living: The Classic Manual on Virtue, Happiness and Effectiveness.* A new interpretation by Sharon Lebell. (New York: HarperCollins, 1994), p.105.

Focussing on the people we are becoming provides a perspective that enables us to walk into the future facing forwards. Certain past regrets or present realities can be rightly built on, but our *focus* ought to be on our future growth. The direction we are facing as leaders makes all the difference. When our focus is driven by who we have been or who we currently are, we will walk into the future facing backwards. When our focus is on the people we are becoming, we can walk into the future facing forwards. There is something wonderfully liberating about this.

Our constant development must imply that we are *not there yet* – we are works in progress. Leadership is not a destination but a journey. The best leaders never stop learning. (We will consider this more in Chapter 46).

In order to help shape the people we are becoming, it is vital we pursue what we are most passionate about. As Steve Jobs, founder of the technology giant *Apple* has said, "*You've got to find what you love*". What we are uniquely passionate about helps us discover our unique purpose. Our passions then act as energisers, enabling us to pursue these passions, even when we face setbacks.

As you consider your unique passions and so discover your unique purpose, try to view this through the lens of 'we' instead of just 'me'. Your purpose will remain short-sighted if it only serves personal interests. Instead, imagine a world where every person discovers their unique purpose that not only energises themselves but also serves those around them. How different a world this would be!

I have often been inspired by the life of former South African President Nelson Mandela. He was a political leader whose life's work was to fight against racial injustice. Mandela spent twenty-seven years in prison, eighteen of those on the infamous Robben Island. In so many ways, these were formative years that shaped the man he was becoming. He had every right to draw attention to himself given how much he suffered, yet he remained inspirationally dedicated to serving others. As he once stated: *"What counts in life is not the mere fact that we have lived. It is the difference we have made in the lives of others that will determine the significance of the life that we lead"*.[2]

How might Mandela's words shape your focus on the person and leader that you are becoming?

Nudges

🖊 When you think about how most movies depict leadership, what images come to mind? What assumptions are embedded in these images? How might they unhelpfully hold you back from appreciating the unique leader that you are becoming?

🖊 If you resolve to walk into the future facing forwards, what regrets from the past might you have to let go of?

🖊 I would encourage you to seek out a leader whom you admire and respect. Ask them to share with you the most significant leadership lesson they have learned. Listen carefully. How can their story help shape the person you are becoming?

---

[2] Cited in Morten T. Hansen, *Great at Work* (London: Simon&Schuster, 2018), p.88.

CHAPTER 5

ONE AMONGST EIGHT BILLION – CELEBRATE THE UNIQUENESS OF YOU

Global populations are currently increasing at a rate of over one percent every year. Based on this trajectory, by 2023 we can expect Planet Earth to be the home of a staggering eight billion people. You are one of them. So am I. What is even more incredible is that not a single one of these eight billion people is the same as another. Not even identical twins have the same fingerprints!

Understanding our uniqueness and identity is vital if we are to appreciate the unique contribution we can bring to this world and specifically to our leadership. Let's consider each for a moment.

Uniqueness

Every individual has a unique set of strengths enabling them to live their life in a unique way. We must resist the tendency to let other people shape us into their version of the person they think we are or ought to be. Learning to acknowledge and celebrate your uniqueness is vital, long before you even lift a finger to lead. Your uniqueness is an ontological reality (it is who you *are* as a person), just as much as your uniqueness is an active reality (shaping what you *do*). Expressing your individuality will enable you to move from your uniqueness of *being* towards your uniqueness of *doing*.

Equally important as a leader is remembering the uniqueness of other team members. Seeking to shape them in our own image is demotivating and potentially damaging. Giving space for others to express themselves creatively and grow into a role is vital. Leaders ought to remember this every time there is a change-over in roles. To assume a new person will approach a role in exactly the same way as the person before them is foolish. Roles may remain the same, but approaches ought to fit the person or people involved. Forgetting this will quickly turn roles into burdens around necks rather than opportunities for unique flourishing.

Identity

Walter Wright helpfully points out in his book, *Relational Leadership,* that *"You don't become a leader by seeking to be a leader but by living out your character."*[3] Appreciating our uniqueness and the uniqueness of others is foundational to developing a robust sense of personal identity. What do you feel are the most common drivers for most people's sense of identity? What are yours? Where leaders look for identity will significantly shape how they lead.

Far too often what we *do* ends up determining our sense of who we *are*. There is an inherent fragility with this. Succeed

---

[3] Walter C. Wright, *Relational Leadership* (London: Authentic Media, 2000), p.114.

and we feel accomplished as a person. Fail and we feel worthless. Leaders are in not immune from this and are, perhaps, most susceptible to it.

Equally, it is all too easy to allow our reputation, or what we *know*, to determine our sense of who we are. Again, there is an inherent fragility with this. When our knowledge and connections take us places, we feel accomplished and significant. When our reputations become marred or our knowledge fails us, we are again left floundering.

By contrast true identity is not rooted in what we *do* or what we *know* but, instead, in who we *are*. Learning to rest with contentment in who we are releases us from having to strive to perform or cover up our failures. When our sense of identity is not determined by our circumstances, it will be far more robust. Learning to find our identity in our being frees us to express our knowing, which in turn fuels our doing. This is foundational for the best leadership.

Remember: there is no-one in the world just like you. You have an utterly unique identity to be embraced and celebrated. It is something to be fought for, both for ourselves and for one another.

Nudges

✎ Spend some time looking at your thumb print and reflecting on how utterly unique it is. What does this tell you about your inherent value?

✎ In what ways are you tempted to let the work that you do define the person that you are? Where have you become more focussed on the *doing* of a leader, at the expense of *being* as a leader?

Write down the names of your three best friends. What unique qualities do they possess? Why not share these encouragements with them when you are next together?

CHAPTER 6

LOOK IN THE MIRROR – IDENTIFY YOUR STRENGTHS, BLIND SPOTS AND AREAS FOR DEVELOPMENT

Strengths

Our unique identities shape the unique ways we display our strengths as leaders. No two people are the same, meaning that no two leaders will ever be the same.

Take for example a character strength such as humility. Two different leaders may possess this same strength, but each leader will exhibit it in a unique way. One person's humility may shine in the quiet example they set, even if they are unaware of how their example touches the lives of others. By contrast, another person's humility may be seen in the way they carry acclaim for the significant contribution they make in a very public role. This person is well-known and well-respected, regularly receiving public praise and recognition. Yet they never use their successes as a means of drawing attention to self. The same strength is utilised in very different ways. Our unique identities shape the unique strengths we have as leaders. What are yours?

Blind spots

Our blind spots are those areas concerning our character or behaviour that are often hidden to us. They can exist for a number of reasons. Perhaps we simply lack self-awareness. Perhaps we are in an environment that has a poor culture of feedback or where those around us are afraid of being honest. This means that our blind spots are given room to develop without being called out, and therefore go unchecked without our knowing. Perhaps we are so focussed on playing to our strengths that we miss the flip side of every strength that plays out in 'bad day' behaviours.

The ability to deliver clear vision is a great strength, but on a bad day can come across as pushy and even arrogant. An ability to consider the opinions of others is a great, but on a bad day can lead to a passivity that shies away from making important calls at the time they are most needed. A keen eye for detail can be a great strength, but on a bad day can lead to negativity or a loss of perspective. Possessing an energy and joy is a great strength, but on a bad day can present as being unrealistic and overbearing.

For each of the following strengths, what might be the possible blind spots?

STRENGTH	POTENTIAL BLIND SPOT
Confident and optimistic	
Logical and analytical	
Conscientious	
Spontaneous	
Decisive and direct	
Structured and steady	
Empathetic and loyal	
Lively and sociable	

Our blind spots might be discovered by ourselves (often becoming apparent after a mistake or a conflict with another person), but more often they will be pointed out by the people around us. When this happens, what is your natural reaction? Can you try and see their comments as a means to your growth?

Areas for development

Our previous two chapters outlined that we are all works in progress. Even our greatest strengths have room for growth. There is always a greater depth of emotional and behavioural maturity to attain to. That said, we will all have some specific areas to develop.

Try to think of two or three blind spots or underdeveloped strengths that you could incorporate into a personal development plan. Use the grid below to work through each, naming specific situations where these areas are relevant,

identifying potential options for change and considering who might be best placed to hold you accountable for your decisions.

Areas for Development	Specific situation of relevance	Potential options for change	Accountability
Example: Area x Can be too direct	Disagreements in meetings	Listen more intentionally, working harder at understanding other points of view	Ask for feedback from meeting Chair for each of the next four meetings
Area 1:			
Area 2:			
Area 3:			

This exercise will help you to be intentional in developing these areas. Notice that the commitments are named, specific, concrete and accountable. Getting in the habit of doing this will go a long way towards meaningful development.

Try to be a leader who regularly looks in the mirror. This is not a vanity exercise! Instead, it should be seen as a positive way to identify and play to strengths, to become aware of blind spots and learn to be more intentional in development. What you do with self-reflection and feedback from others is mission-critical to how you develop as a leader.

Nudges

How do you *want* to be perceived as a leader? How do you think you *are* perceived as a leader? What could you do to begin addressing any gap?

Are your blind spots most commonly discovered by yourself or pointed out by others? What might be the advantages and disadvantages of each?

As you consider your areas for development, what positive difference would it make to a) your leadership and b) those around you, if you were to grow consistently in these areas?

CHAPTER 7

BITTER OR BETTER - PUT FAILURE INTO PERSPECTIVE

Resilience is a bit of a buzz word these days and for good reason. The world is a tough place to live in, let alone lead in. Resilience will help us to cope better with this. Resilience is the ability to bounce back from difficulties and like a muscle, is built over time with exercise. Building resilience shows us that the only real mistakes we make are the ones we fail to learn from. Consider the following examples:

Dame Ellen MacArthur (former yacht racer and winner of BBC's *Sport's Personality of the Year*) writes in her stimulating 2002 autobiography, *Taking on the World*,[4] about the depths she was taken to physically and emotionally during her famous *Vende Globe* yacht race which she completed single-handedly aged just twenty-four. Her example of resilience is deeply inspirational.

---

[4] Ellen MacArthur, *Taking on the World* (London: Penguin Books, 2002).

Ant Middleton (ex-Special Forces sniper and former star of Channel 4's *SAS: Who Dares Wins*) says that *"failure isn't making the mistake but allowing the mistake to win."*[5] Through the adversity of fighting on the front line over many years, he has developed great resilience. Failure has helped him get to know himself better.

Ken Allen (former CEO of the logistics company *DHL)* delivered (excuse the pun!) one of the biggest turnarounds in transport history. The inspirational story is told in his book *Radical Simplicity*[6] and the leadership lessons at the end of each chapter are well worth digesting. He never saw mistakes as failures as long as they provided opportunities to be better next time.

Michael Jordan (former NBA[7] professional) is still considered by many fans to be the greatest basket player of all time. He has often pointed out in media interviews that he missed over nine thousand shots in his career. The key to his resilience was what he learnt from these misses. Indeed, it was the shots he missed that he used to his advantage to train himself for the 32,292 NBA points he *did* score.

Tanni Grey-Thompson (Former Paralympic wheelchair athlete) regularly speaks on the subject of disability discrimination and the resilience she has needed and continues to need, in order to overcome unhelpful and patronising comments people make to her.

Sir Ernest Shackleton (20th Century Antarctic explorer) was a hugely successful leader, despite the fact that he failed to

---

[5] Ant Middleton, *First Man In* (London: Harper Collins, 2018), p.175.
[6] Ken Allen, *Radical Simplicity* (London: Ebury Press, 2019).
[7] National Basketball Association.

reach nearly every goal he set. His greatest failure in terms of exploration was probably his *Endurance* expedition across the Antarctic from 1914-1916. The voyage ended in disaster, but Shackleton miraculously brought his entire team home to safety under the most unlikely conditions. He never reached his goal, but his success is rooted in the person he became through this experience and the transformation in the people he led. Optimism was one of his great hallmarks and there is much we can learn from the way he led. Perhaps most notable is that when he didn't reach his goals, he never gave up.

These examples illustrate that resilience is not only an ability but also an attitude that seeks to turn failures or significant challenges into positive advantages. When this happens, our failures and challenges can become potent fuel for positive change. The key in all of this is having the right mindset.

You might find it helpful to consider the following diagram:

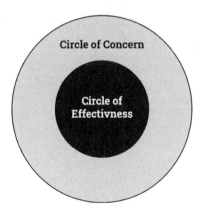

Each set of unique circumstances we face in life will cause us to see and experience a range of concerns. These can be both perceived and actual threats and, taken together, could be called our *Circle of Concern*. For each of these concerns there will be elements we can control, elements we can influence and elements we can do nothing about.

The key to developing resilience is to focus on the areas we can control (in reality these are often very few) and the elements we can influence (perhaps a few more). Together these could be called our *Circle of Effectiveness*.

Surprisingly, the more we focus on things we *cannot* have any control or influence over, the smaller our *Circle of Effectiveness* becomes. Conversely, the more we focus on things we *can* control or have influence over, the bigger our *Circle of Effectiveness* becomes.

As we have already seen, we must know ourselves well in order to lead ourselves well. Understanding these two circles will help us. We need to learn which elements within our *Circle of Concern* have the greatest potential to cause us stress and then intentionally seek to look at those concerns through the lens of our *Circle of Effectiveness*. What *can* we control or have influence over? Focussing on our *Circle of Effectiveness* will dampen our stress-triggers, ground our situation in greater perspective, and help us develop our resilience muscles.

Our failures and mistakes don't have to define who we are as people. In fact, they ought not to. The test we go through can become our testimony – a story to encourage others. The mess we learn from can become our message – a story to inspire others. Keep speaking positivity to yourself and to others, never allowing past failures to paralyse you. Former US Secretary of State, Henry Kissinger, once made a remark about 'a diamond being a chunk of coal that did well under pressure.' Maybe it is time to put your mistakes and failures into perspective in a similar way.

Nudges

- When you face setbacks, does this lead you immediately to want to manage everything more carefully? What might be the downsides to this?

- Try to identify a person whom you respect for their resilience in the face of setbacks. Why not ask to spend some time with them and try to learn all you can.

- Think about the biggest challenge you are currently facing. How might the Circle of Concern and the Circle of Effectiveness help you to regain perspective and turn the challenge into an opportunity for personal growth?

CHAPTER 8

REACH FOR THE STARS - DARE TO DREAM

One of the reasons that the *Disney* film makers have seen such enduring success since their 1923 founding year is the way they consistently harness the power of imagination. Their mission statement speaks in part of a desire to *'inspire people around the globe through the power of unparalleled storytelling'.*[8]

This ability to inspire others is one of the marks of a leader. So too is the ability to dare to dream and then go after those dreams.

We saw back in Chapter 6 that our unique identities shape the unique strengths we have as leaders. When these strengths are combined with the strengths of others and then together channelled into an inspiring vision, great things can happen. To help you grow as a leader, giving yourself permission to dream, here are four things to reflect on:

---

[8] The Walt Disney Company. *"About the Walk Disney Company"*. www.thewaltdisneycompany.com/about/. Accessed 19th January 2021.

Know your strengths and the unique contribution that you alone can make

It is all too easy as leaders to spend too much of our lives pursuing the dreams or expectation of others, rather than listening to our own heartbeat. Instead of striving to be the leader that you are not, try to channel your energy into the unique leader that you *are*. What are your particular strengths? What unique contribution are you bringing to bear on the situation in front of you? No one else can lead into this situation in exactly the same way as you.

Avoid listening to negative voices

Inspirational leadership will inevitably be met by negative voices. Of course there can be wisdom in some of these voices and we need to learn to be discerning. Yet, be aware that a voice of caution or indeed opposition can quickly destroy inspiration if it is misplaced. We need to learn to discern what is a wise word of warning and filter this from the array of unnecessary negativity that often surrounds us. Negativity saps energy, deflates creativity and destroys vision. It is also important to check our own hearts as leaders. How are you getting on in the negativity-positivity stakes? How much of the influence you have over others is fuelled by negativity instead of positivity?

Seize opportunities

Barak Obama, the former US President, once said that *"change will not come if we wait for some other person or some other time."*[9] Seizing opportunities is about being bold when

---

[9] From a pre-election speech to supporters after the February 5th 2008 nominating contests. The full transcript can be viewed at: www.nytimes.com/2008/02/05/us/politics/05text-obama.html. Accessed 21 February 2021.

they are placed before us. It is about creating the future we want to see rather than expecting someone else to do this. Although patience might be the next step, perhaps now is the best time to act. But not always. Seizing opportunities should never be about making rash decisions or being cavalier in our outlook. Change for change's sake is a form of leadership-fidgeting and should be avoided. Seizing opportunities is more about allowing the energy that fuels inspiration and dreams to keep on flowing. As has often been quipped in professional sport: *You miss one hundred percent of the shots you do not take.*

Challenge the status quo

Leadership often involves stepping into the unknown, treading where no one had trodden before. This takes courage. Having a robust and rooted sense of self (truly knowing ourselves) is vital for being prepared to challenge for a better way. Without this, we will end up being leaders who are like rudderless ships, tossed around by the winds and waves of other people's opinions and approaches.

You are unique. This makes you a unique leader. Never let anyone steal this fact from you. Give yourself permission to dream!

Nudges

✎   Remind yourself of the content of Chapter 4 (who you are becoming) and Chapter 5 (uniqueness). How could reflecting on your uniqueness shape the way you dream about the future? What are you most passionate about? How could you turn this passion into action that would serve other people?

- Most people are motivated by either a 'need to achieve' or a 'need to avoid failure'. Which is most true of you? How might this shape the way you go after your dreams?

- If you could change one thing in the world that would impact other people for good, what would it be? What is the biggest defeater belief that is holding you back from pursuing this dream?

PART 2

LEADING YOURSELF

"Before you are a leader, success is all about grow-ing yourself. When you become a leader, success is all about growing others."

Jack Welch – Former CEO
General Electric

Effective leadership starts with ourselves. Taking responsibility for oneself is often far more demand-ing than taking responsibility for others. Self-leader-ship is probably the greatest challenge that any leader will face. It calls us to play to our strengths, grow out of our weaknesses and be open to being shown our blind spots. By learning to lead ourselves well, we will develop a firm foundation on which to lead others.

CHAPTER 9

INNER FOUNDATIONS – THIS THING CALLED CHARACTER

The best leaders have learnt the discipline of leading themselves well. This starts not with what we do but with who we are. We have to know ourselves well (Part 1) if we are to lead ourselves well (Part 2). Such leaders have an unshakable inner foundation that lies at the heart of who they are. It's this thing called character.

Leadership has often been characterised by the 4 C's:

Convictions – motivational values that shape vision

Competency – the ability to perform tasks at the highest level

Chemistry – shared values and practices that unite and brings relational life

Character – the mental and moral qualities that distinctively underpin an individual

It is easy in leadership to become transfixed by the first three and unconsciously overlook the fourth. Yet character is the attribute that in many ways underpins all the others. Whilst it may be true that people of genius will be admired, people of wealth envied and people of power feared, only people of character will be trusted. Developing the inner foundation of character that is so fundamental to being trusted is *the* key to leading ourselves well.

What are the character traits you most admire in other people? Humility? Integrity? Sincerity? Patience? Positivity? Kindness? Self-control? Loyalty? Each of these traits (and no doubt others you have thought of) all take time to develop. There is a necessary maturity to true character that demonstrates it has not been forged overnight. Most often it is developed through trial, challenge and the all-important ingredient: time. As someone once quipped: *'Character grows in a crockpot.'*

Let's consider the examples given above:

> Humility – developed over time through a continual choice to reject pride
>
> Integrity – forged through exposure to situations that tempt dishonesty
>
> Sincerity – grown steadily by rejecting falsehood and fakery
>
> Patience – moulded through endurance and frustration
>
> Positivity – fought for when negativity commonly pervades
>
> Kindness – motivated by a distaste for selfishness

Self-control – carved through experiencing the consequences of foolishness

Loyalty – developed through a costly commitment to a meaningful person or cause

Character runs deep, which is why it deeply matters. In many ways, our characters display the heart of who we are as people.

Just as the character traits above are positive and to be commended, there are also negative character traits that true leadership ought to avoid. Traits such as impatience, selfishness, pride, dishonesty and negativity. Notice how each of these, in contrast to the life-giving character traits shown previously, can be produced quickly. Rather than being forged through challenge, they are often the product of choosing the easy path.

Again, some examples:

Impatience – wanting the easy option and seeking it immediately

Selfishness – thinking of self at the expense of serving another

Pride – thinking too lowly or too highly of self (often driven by unhelpful comparison to others)

Dishonesty – choosing to cover up mistakes or exaggerate successes in order to promote self

Negativity – looking to blame others or stand on personal rights when challenged

Imagine you have in your hand a tube of toothpaste. When you squeeze it, toothpaste comes out. Our character is like a tube of toothpaste – when we are squeezed, what is inside of us will come out. The all-important question to ask ourselves therefore is this: *what sort of character will come out of me?*

Character is the foundation stone for leading ourselves well and, in so many ways, it is the litmus test for true leadership, making it something worth investing in and guarding at all costs.

Nudges

🖊 What is it about your character that you are most thankful for? How could you best use this to serve other people as you lead?

🖊 How have the challenges you have faced in your life helped to deepen this character trait in you?

🖊 In what area of your life are you most in danger of putting development of you competency ahead of your character?

CHAPTER 10

SWEEP THE SHEDS - HUMILITY AND THE BURYING OF EGO

The New Zealand All Blacks rugby team has been one of the most successful and consistent teams in modern sport, winning three of the last eight World Cups. One of the key characteristics of this team is the emphasis placed on the character and the personal discipline of each player. If you are skilfully one of the best players, but you lack character, you never get picked. To the All Blacks, character triumphs over talent.

One of the most well-known sayings associated with this team is *Sweep the Sheds.* The idea is that a player must never think they are too important to do the small things that need to be done. The All Blacks take it in turns to clean out the changing room after training. There are no 'Captain's Privileges'. *Every* player takes their turn. There is no place for egos.

Think of the ego a bit like a target we carry around on our chest. The bigger it is, the more vulnerable we are to getting hit. A large ego is more open to manipulation since it craves attention. It can make us less open to learning and less able to say sorry. A large ego also narrows our vision because it strengthens a confirmation bias, allowing us to hear or see only things we like. Egos are more concerned with protecting personal reputations than facing up to personal shortcomings.

Crucial to leading ourselves well is always maintaining a humble attitude, deliberately burying our egos. Humble leaders own their inability and shortcomings, taking responsibility when things go wrong. There is no felt need to cover weaknesses up. Humble leaders also feel no need to draw attention to their successes. As the Maori saying goes: '*Waiho mā te tangata e mibi*' – 'Let someone else praise your virtues'.

This isn't saying that we should not take satisfaction in personal transformation and achievement, but that we should not seek to draw attention to ourselves. On the other hand, a person who overly plays down a significant achievement might be expressing false humility. Pride can be fuelled by thinking of ourselves more highly that we ought, but so too can thinking of ourselves too lowly. As pastor Tim Keller writes, "*humility is not thinking more of myself or thinking less of myself, it is thinking of myself less.*"[10] Ultimately it is an issue of focus - who is the spotlight on? Truly humble leaders do not feel the need to draw attention to themselves.

---

[10] Tim Keller, Personal Tweet on Twitter - *@timkellernyc*. September 20, 2019.

In *The 360 Leader,* best-selling author, John Maxwell, writes about the difference between Self-Promotion and Selfless- Promotion[11]:

Self-Promotion	Vs	Selfless Promotion
Me First		Others first
Move up		Build up
Guard information		Share information
Take Credit		Give credit
Hog the ball (star)		Pass the ball (enable others to star)
Dodge the ball (blame)		Share the ball (take responsibility)
Manipulate others		Motivate others

A little reflection over these differences is a worthwhile exercise for all leaders. Which area of self-promotion are you most prone to? Remember: the greatest danger to your life as a leader lives inside you, not outside.

The best leaders display a robust mix of three attributes:

1. I - Influence (the ability to take people with you)
2. A - Ability (skill to lead effectively and get tasks done)
3. H - Humility (a self-less view of oneself)

Consider the relationship between all three. What happens if one is missing?

---

[11] John C. Maxwell, *The 360° Leader*, Chapter 4 *The Ego Challenge* (Nashville: Nelson Business, 2005), p. 55.

I + A (but no H)   = leaders who achieve but sometimes at cost to others

I + H (but no A)   = leaders who are likeable but incompetent

A + H (but no I)   = leaders of limited impact

What might the result be if all three were combined?

I + A + H = Effective leadership

This is what we ought to aspire towards.

Nudges

✐ *"Humility is not thinking more of myself or less of myself; it is thinking of myself less."* Try and put this quote from Tim Keller in your own words.

✐ Think of a leader who exemplifies humility. What about them in particular do you find attractive?

✐ Try to identity a relationship or situation in your life in which you are conscious that your ego can easily become enlarged, causing damage to yourself and others. Who might hold you accountable in this?

CHAPTER 11

TAKING OFF THE MASK - PRIVATE AND PUBLIC LIVES THAT ALIGN

We have seen that leading ourselves well involves developing robust character and humility. Leading ourselves well also involves authenticity (fostering credibility and trust) and integrity (private and public lives matching up). Taken together, these four become a rock-solid foundation for leadership. Whom do you know who exemplifies these qualities?

In the first century, one of the primary means of entertainment was found in theatre. Often these theatres were outdoor spaces where crowds gathered to watch various actors perform. They were called *Hypocrites*, from the Greek word *'hypokrite'* which means actor. They often wore large masks to denote the characters they played and interchanging these masks was a means of playing multiple roles.

Have you noticed how we can do something similar in our own lives? Often driven by insecurity and a desire for recognition or affirmation, we wear various 'masks' to disguise the • real us. Social media can be used powerfully in this way by affording us a freedom to portray a side of ourselves that we are comfortable for others to see, whilst masking the other side that we would prefer to hide. We want people to see our successes, but not our failures. We want people to see our strengths, but not our weaknesses. We want people to think well of us, so we hide our inadequacies. Wear these masks long enough and we even start to believe the lie that they create.

Interestingly, influences such as insecurity, pride and fear can undermine the foundation for solid leadership described above. Character is replaced with fickleness. Humility with pride. Authenticity is replaced with performance. Integrity with falsehood. The irony is that we can put on masks, believing people will think well of us, when in reality they are more drawn to the authentic us when our masks are taken off.

Another way to look at this is to acknowledge that we all have a Front Stage and a Back Stage. The Front Stage is where the performance takes place. This is what we like people to see and we have great freedom to shape what people see. The Front Stage is the place where we often try to hold it all together. We think vulnerability and weakness have no place here. Our Back Stage, by comparison, is the real us, but importantly not the us that people most see. We have less freedom to shape our Back Stage because it is where the more honest version of us resides. Our successes *and* our failures can be seen here: the us that we like *and* the us we dislike.

Constantly living on the Front Stage and wearing these metaphorical masks is exhausting. We portray an image of ourselves and our leadership that is not an honest reflection of the people we truly are. Leadership built on a lie will soon be exposed.

In order to address this identity conflict, we need help in removing the masks. Accountability is perhaps the most effective means, by having someone in our life who knows us well enough and cares about us deeply enough to speak truth to us. We must remember, however, that the key in making accountability meaningful is ourselves. We've got to want it when it challenges us as much as when it affirms us.

If you are aware of a particular area of weakness or personal challenge, try thinking of the question that you do not want someone else to ask you. Identify this question and then ask your accountability partner to ensure they ask it regularly! This may not be easy but is one of the most powerful ways of learning to take off our masks and grow in areas we might not have otherwise seen. Consistency between our private lives (what people may not see) and public lives (what people will see) is vital if we are to lead with integrity.

Nudges

- What masks are you aware of putting on in your life? What drives this?

- Who are you accountable to? How have they helped you grow?

- What one question do you *not* want them to ask you?

CHAPTER 12

WORDS OF WISDOM AND WOE - THE POWER OF SELF-TALK

Each of us possesses a powerful weapon that can be used for good or for evil. This weapon may be small, but it carries great influence. Any idea what it is?

The words of other people can have huge influence over us, but it is the words that we speak to ourselves that can have the greatest impact of all. A key discipline therefore in leading ourselves well is guarding our self-talk.

Have you ever stopped to think about how you speak to yourself?

The words we speak to ourselves (even when they are not true) can profoundly shape how we view ourselves, how we view situations and how we view relative successes and failures. Our self-talk holds the power therefore to be hugely destructive but also wonderfully constructive. We can speak folly and falsehood or wisdom and truth. The choice is ours.

When it comes to the challenges that we will inevitably face as leaders, it is easy to feel overwhelmed. (We will consider this more in Chapter 14 when we look at leadership and stress.) Stress can influence the way we speak to ourselves. Here are two suggestions that can profoundly shape our self-talk in a positive way.

The first involves identifying and dealing with our limiting beliefs. These are beliefs we regularly speak to ourselves that can allow fear to dominate and paralyse us. Limiting beliefs are normally articulated verbally or subconsciously in the phrase: "*I can't ...... because ....*".

> "*I can't keep going .... because I've lost all my confidence.*"
>
> "*I can't ask for help .... because they will think I'm weak.*"
>
> "*I can't figure this out .... because it has all got too messy.*"
>
> "*I can't change my behaviour .... because it has gone on for too long.*"
>
> "*I can't change this situation .... because I've not got the influence.*"

Whilst each of these statements may be felt acutely and are legitimate *feelings*, none of them is objectively true. Here is why.

Maybe our confidence is shot, such that we cannot keep going. But there are things we *can* do to re-build our confidence.

Maybe we feel that asking for help will expose our weaknesses.

Yet drawing upon the strength of another person may be the very thing we need to learn to be stronger leaders together.

Maybe our situation has become so messy that our current mode of thinking prevents us from figuring it out.

Yet we can invite different perspectives that may help us see the situation differently.

Maybe we feel our own destructive behaviours have gone on too long and are out of hand.

Yet perhaps all we need is a fresh environment that will inspire us towards lasting change.

Maybe we feel we lack influence and therefore cannot change a situation.

Yet perhaps the very leadership strength that is needed is to step sideways, acknowledging that someone else is better placed to display influence.

Limiting beliefs are exactly that: beliefs that limit. If we change the way we speak to ourselves, we can change the way we think, see, and believe, and the limits that once held us fast can be removed. New possibilities then begin to emerge.

The second means of profoundly re-shaping our self-talk in a positive way is through the practice of reframing. This is a means of regaining control over swamped emotions. Imagine the challenging situation in front of you is captured inside a photo frame. Your focus hones in on what is inside this frame and you begin trying to unscramble the mess and make sense of it all. The more you stare at the contents within the frame, the messier it seems. You soon become overwhelmed. At this point, imagine you are handed a new photo frame. This one is far larger, taking in more information, fresh perspective and greater context. Looking at your circumstances through this new frame completely alters what you see and the way you seek to process it. The key to this practice is remembering that your circumstances have not changed. What has changed is your perspective, simply through the means of reframing.

Try to differentiate between your emotions and your behaviours. *Both* matter but we need to avoid excusing unhelpful thought-patterns and behaviours despite the inevitability of troubled emotions. As leaders, we must learn to guard our self-talk. This is vital if we are to overcome limiting beliefs and master the art of reframing.

Nudges

✐ What limiting beliefs most hold you back from becoming the person you want to be?

✐ What would be the most constructive thing you could say to your best friend to strengthen their self-talk?

✐ In what area of your life are you most prone to feeling overwhelmed? How might the exercise of reframing help you regain control of your swamped emotions?

CHAPTER 13

BEWARE THE TIPPING POINT - LEADERSHIP AND STRESS

One of the greatest challenges of leadership is developing enough resilience to help us handle stress. Becoming aware of our triggers for stress and how these play out is a vital discipline to master.

Every leader has a capacity and every leader's capacity will differ from the next person's. Our capacity is the load we can carry without reaching our tipping point. If we find ourselves on the wrong side of our tipping point, stress begins to build, lowering our tolerance levels. Eventually we reach a point when stress becomes unmanageable and we start doing very real damage to ourselves and those around us. Normally this is evidenced in poor judgement and decision-making.

Although stress can be induced in a moment (an unforeseen crisis for instance), it more commonly develops as an accumulation of pressure. In order to avoid this, here are three suggested *D*'s to consider as a leader, each of which can help keep inevitable stress contained: Derailers, De-stressors and Discernment.

Derailers

These are emotional triggers or specific circumstances which possess great power to catch us out. What are you most vulnerable to? What situation or relationship most easily presses the wrong button for you? When are you aware of having reduced tolerance levels? We need to become more aware of these situations if we are to learn to overcome them.

Consider for a moment the various phases of a typical day. Most of us have a best time when we feel fresh and can think most clearly. This is when we typically make our best decisions. By contrast, we probably also have our worst time when we are often weary, less responsive and in danger of making poor decisions. Being self-aware of these times is crucial to leading ourselves well.

So too is building margin into each day. Margin is the space between our load and our limits. Too many leaders pack each day close to or beyond their capacity. In the short term this may seem productive, but it will not be long before we reach our tipping point and stress pushes us over the edge. Not only are we then no longer productive, but we have moved to a place from which it will take us far longer to recover productiveness. Building margin into our days may feel counter-productive but is essential if we are to avoid our derailers.

De-stressors

These are things that help us relax and most naturally reduce stress that might otherwise build up in the background. (We would be wise to find life-giving de-stressors; not all activities that can relax us are necessarily good for us!) It has often been said it is not the amount of stress we are under that is the key to coping, but having de-stressors built into our lives. We will think about this more in Chapter 15. De-stressors are a vital tonic to alleviating the inevitable stress that leadership involves. Without them our tolerance levels will become hugely reduced. With them we will probably find we can absorb far greater volumes of stress because the stress never ends up pushing us beyond our tipping point.

Discernment

This is a crucial skill for every leader. Discernment involves learning when to say *"no"*. This enables us to establish healthy boundaries. What we *don't* focus on as leaders matters in many ways more than what we *do* focus on. This is because every time we say *"no"* to something we are then freed to say *"yes"* to something else.

In his best-selling book *The Seven Habits of Highly Effective People,* Steven Covey talks about seeking to find your inner peace as a leader. He suggests that this is when your schedule and values are aligned such that you do not prioritise what is on your schedule, but instead schedule your priorities.[12] Without keeping a tight eye on our values, our schedules become crammed with urgent tasks that crowd out important ones. Having lost the ability to say *"no,"* we have little or no capacity to say *"yes"* to better things. To help combat this, try creating a *'not-to-do list'* this week. You'll be amazed at how it helps you to stay focussed.

Being aware of our derailers, building in de-stressors and cultivating discernment are crucial skills for any leader looking to flourish when under stress.

---

[12] Steven R. Covey, *7 Habits of Highly Effective People,* Habit 3 Put First Things First (London: Simon & Schuster, 2004), p. 161.

Nudges

✎ Spend some time trying to identify potential derailers to your leadership. Naming them is half the battle in overcoming them.

✎ How do you best de-stress? How could you build these things into the rhythm of a) each day, b) each week, c) each month?

✎ If you were to create a '*not*-to-do list', what would be the first thing to go on it?

CHAPTER 14

CHEERLEADERS AND CHALLENGERS - NEVER LEADING ALONE

Not only does a leader need to face up to and overcome stress (see Chapter 13), but many also find that leadership can be lonely. This can be the case even when we lead in team environments. Part of this loneliness can come through the responsibility carried by a leader and the sense that few, if any others, really 'get' some of the pressures you may legitimately feel. But another part of this loneliness is the leader's own making. Leadership becomes isolating only when a leader isolates themselves. A leader can become isolated by trying to solve problems singlehandedly, failing to listen to those around them, or forgetting their own blind spots or need for personal growth.

A key to leading ourselves well is never to place ourselves in a situation where we are leading alone. We need each other. Every leader needs at least one challenger and one cheerleader. Let's look at each in turn.

Cheerleaders

These are people who naturally energise us. They help lift our heads and inspire us to keep going. Cheerleaders are sources of positivity. They help develop healthy mindsets within us. If something is possible, even vaguely possible, the cheerleader will remind us that this is so! They are most often people who know us well enough to be able to speak timely and wise words into our lives. Never play down the power of encouragement. Effective leaders are great encouragers and effective leaders have great encouragers in their own lives. Think for a moment who yours may be.

Challengers

Every leader also needs challengers. Whilst it may feel nice to be surrounded by cheerleaders, leadership also requires challenge. We need to be held accountable. We need people who can see the blind spots that we might not readily see in ourselves. We need people who can help lift us out of the echo chambers it is all too easy to get stuck in, where we become insulated from rebuttal, only hearing the things we want to hear. We need challengers who care about us enough to tell us honestly what they see, in order that we might grow. Just as effective leaders are wise in the challenges they offer to others, so effective leaders need challengers in their own lives. Think for a moment who yours may be.

In situations where you are a challenger to someone else, the feedback you provide is vital to their growth. Giving quality feedback, however, is not easy. Few of us are good at giving it and few of us are good at receiving it. Feedback can catch people off guard if the timing is wrong. Bring all these challenges together and we soon realise our need to work at our feedback intentionally if we are to be effective challengers.

If a particularly strong challenge is needed, it can be wise to anchor the challenge in the agreed values of your team or organisation. This makes the challenge more objective and part of a wider vision. Think too of ways in which to match appropriate challenge with encouragement – every leader needs support. Try to frame challenge in a relational context as opposed to a confrontational one.

Often our cheerleaders and challengers are people older and wiser than us, those who have already been where we currently are. The encouragement from both often comes with perspective and experience.

Cheerleaders might say: *"Don't give up! It may seem like you're not making progress, but that was my experience. Keep persevering. The breakthrough will come."*

Challengers might say: *"Guard your attitude in this frustrating situation. I sense you are beginning to lose control. I failed in this area when I was leading in your role and it caused a great deal of damage. I want to help you avoid the mistakes I made."*

The experience, perspective and wisdom of the years are invaluable. However, it is also worth considering the help you could be given by someone younger than you. Whilst an *older* cheerleader or challenger may be able to bring their experience, a *younger* cheerleader or challenger might bring fresh insight. You don't always need to have experience to have valuable insight. Indeed, experience can cloud genuine insight if it is stuck in repeated patterns of thinking and behaviour.

Perhaps it is time for you to consider finding a mentor who is younger than you, rather than blindly following the traditional model and assuming mentors always ought to be older. This may take humility on your part and a maturity and confidence on theirs, but it could become the key that deepens your leadership.

Nudges

✎ Think of two people in your life, one who would be your best challenger and the other who would be your best cheerleader. Ask the challenger to show you a blind spot to work on. Ask the cheerleader to encourage you in one area in which they have seen you grow as a leader in the last year.

✎ Few people have a mentor younger than they are. How might having a younger mentor add value to the way you currently lead?

✎ Think of a person for whom you could become a challenger or a cheerleader. What intentional steps could you take to help that person?

CHAPTER 15

KEEP YOUR BUCKET FULL – LEADING WITH PASSION

Imagine for a moment that you are a bucket! Strange ask, I know, but run with it for a moment. When we begin leading, it may feel like we are a shiny new bucket, so filled with passion that nothing can stop us. It's a lovely place to be, but over time the bucket becomes worn. Cracks begin to appear; pressure increases and gradually our leadership passion begins to leak away. The thing about these cracks is that they are not always easy to spot. Passion can slowly leak away without us consciously being aware of it. Sometimes we only spot the problem when our bucket is nearly empty, which may be too late for the necessary repairs. Leading can be really tough and some seasons can feel like a real grind. Maintaining passion for what we do is vital if we are to keep going in these darker days.

The most effective leaders have a passion for the cause or the people they are leading and have learnt to sustain that passion by regularly refilling their bucket. Too many leaders treat burn out (the empty bucket) like a badge of honour. It may seem virtuous to wear yourself out for your cause, but leaders who get to that place soon stagnate or, even worse, become a liability. These dangers can be avoided by finding the things that inspire us and using them regularly to refill our passion bucket.

What inspires you? It is amazing how our mood (and subsequent passion) can be significantly influenced by simple things such as a hearty meal, sitting before a beautiful sunset, listening to a favourite piece of music or reading a stimulating book. Are you a leader who knows *what* inspires you, and do you regularly go after these things in order to keep your passion bucket full?

Who inspires you? Who are those energisers who always leave you feeling refreshed and enthused? Who are the people who have a knack of reframing your perspectives and opening your eyes to better ways of approaching things? Are you a leader who knows *who* inspires you? Do you regularly spend time under their influence? These are vital questions to ask in order to keep our passion buckets full.

Where inspires you? Place can be significant. Place evokes memories and can draw out the best in us. Place can move us to more inspired thinking. Sometimes it is choosing to work *in* a particular place. Other times, it is choosing to withdraw from work *to* a particular place. Are you a leader who knows *where* inspires you and regularly chooses to go there in order to keep your passion bucket full?

Taking time to consider your *what*, *who* and *where* can help you make a regular habit of bucket refilling rather than merely wishing you had the time to do so. To many busy leaders it can feel counter-intuitive to take time out from leading others in order to lead themselves better. But it is always time well spent. Sustaining vision is very hard when we are tired, and it is nearly impossible to lead others well when we are not growing ourselves.

There will be times as a leader where you complete a task ahead of schedule, thus handing yourself a time dividend. Have you ever stopped to consider how you spend this? The most natural response is to plough it back into more activity, either getting ahead in the next task or seeking to deliver the current task to an even higher level. Whilst there may be occasions when this is wise, perhaps the less obvious but more effective response would be to spend your time dividend investing in you. Try to learn the discipline of enjoying the margin, rather than insisting the time must be spent productively. Perhaps you could read an extra chapter in a book to help shape your decision-making approach, rather than just make the next decision. Perhaps you could sit still with your favourite drink and appreciate the small things in life that can be easily overlooked.

Time dividends can be vital gifts for refilling our passion bucket. How intentional are you in how you use yours?

Nudges

🖋 What hobbies or relationships are most life-giving to you? How much of a priority is it for you to regularly invest in these things?

🖋 What is the worst attribute that comes out of you when you are exhausted? As you reflect on this, how does it influence the importance of learning

🖋 When you complete a task earlier than expected, how do you typically spend your time dividend?

CHAPTER 16

DON'T BE A SHEEP – LEAD WITH COURAGE

We are living and leading at an unprecedented time of global history where so many economic, social and environmental challenges are colliding simultaneously. It often feels like the skies are growing darker, yet challenges present opportunities, making this a great time to be a leader. The world needs leaders right now like never before.

As we wrap up Part 2 (Leading Yourself), we need to consider what it takes to lead with courage. Courage starts with the resolve to be a leader and not a sheep! Here are two observations about sheep: firstly, sheep follow other sheep, and secondly, sheep are only interested in what is under their nose. To be a courageous leader, we need to learn to do the opposite.

Leaders need to lead. This may sound obvious but far too many leaders stop leading, wandering like sheep following sheep, or even becoming paralysed by fear or apathy. A courageous leader is a leader who thinks deeply, listens carefully and then is prepared to buck the trends in order to pursue something better.

Leaders also need to keep looking forward and this takes great courage. It is tempting to settle down in the comfort of the field you are currently grazing in rather than looking for where you are going next. It is challenging to keep an eye out for new opportunities as well as for dangers. It takes great courage to do the right thing instead of opting for the easy thing.

What may be holding you back from being a more courageous leader? Perhaps it is the fear of other people, not wishing to unsettle anyone. Perhaps it is the knowledge that change requires effort. Perhaps it is the paralysis of analysis – wanting

to control every detail and allowing repeated conversations as a means of avoiding having to make a decision.

If we are going to learn to be leaders instead of sheep and lead with courage and not fear, here are three suggestions to consider:

Firstly, sheep are stubborn; leaders are flexible. Courageous leaders recognise that an approach that led to success in the past may not lead to success in the future. You may have entered a field through one gate, but it may be prudent to leave through another. Asking 'W*hy*? and '*What if*?' takes the courage that pushes for the best outcome, not just the easiest one.

Secondly, sheep keep their heads down; leaders keep their heads up. Courageous leaders are not afraid to lift their heads to observe what is going on around and be prepared to make the hard decision to move to another field. With our focus constantly on the task, we miss the gift of perspective which is so often needed to help us pursue better opportunities and to avoid danger. Courageous leadership will inevitably bring with it a dose of disappointment, setback and failure. The ability to keep our own heads up and inspire this same attitude in those around us will be one litmus test for effective leadership.

Thirdly, sheep follow the flock; leaders lead the flock. Courageous leaders are prepared to do the right thing for the right reasons, even when it is costly to do so. This involves combining courage with discipline. The courageous leader commits to show up day in, day out, especially in situations they cannot predict or control. Consider the following leadership arithmetic:

Wrong thing for wrong reason = disaster

Wrong thing for right reason = lacks impact

Right thing for wrong reason = lacks integrity

Right thing for right reason = courageous leadership

We are living in an era full of challenge and fear. Take heart! This is a great time to be a leader who leads with courage. This starts with leading ourselves well.

Nudges

- Think of an example where you have shown courage to do the right thing for the right reason. What was the impact on a) you? and b) others?

- What is the primary barrier that holds you back from being more courageous as a leader?

- Seek out a leader whom you respect. Ask them to share with you examples of when they have had to show courage. What do you learn?

PART 3

UNDERSTANDING OTHERS

"If one does not understand a person, one tends to regard him as a fool."

Carl Jung
Swiss Psychologist (20th Century)

Understanding other people is a great skill to master for without this, it's impossible to help bring out the best in them. Understanding others requires us to be observant and to commit to a posture of listening. Understanding others requires us to be sensitive to how others might feel in a certain situation and to be more in tune with how they might think. This puts us in a far better place to understand their reactions, which enables us to communicate more effectively.

CHAPTER 17

WHEN SMART IS STUPID – BECOMING MORE SELF-AWARE

The American philosopher William James once said that, whenever two people meet, there are really six people present: there is each person as they see themself, each as the other person sees them and each as they really are.[13] For this reason, becoming more self-aware is a vital skill for anyone seeking to be an effective leader.

There was once a student at school who was considered by her teachers to be a genius. Let's call the student Lucy. She often corrected the mistakes of her maths teacher and the running joke was that she was brighter than he was. She had a phenomenal IQ (Intelligence Quotient).

For centuries, IQ, which measures reasoning and problem-solving skills, has been deemed to be *the* marker for

---

[13] Cited in: Mark R. Luborsky and Andrea P. Sankar, *The Interrogative Imperative: State, Community and Individual as Bodies and Subjectives.* Medical Anthropology Medical Quarterly, 2009, June; 23(2): 89-90.

intelligence, despite people like the Greek philosopher, Aristotle, being interested in emotional skilfulness. Only in 1995 did EQ (Emotional Quotient), a measure of emotional intelligence, begin to be popularised due to the influence of Daniel Goleman.[14] From this point on, EQ has been viewed as an equally important form of intelligence. Indeed, many people see it as *more* important.

Back in 2016, the World Economic Forum published its *Future of Jobs Report*.[15] This report predicted that, by 2020, Emotional Intelligence would be the second most sought after skill for employees. The report also drew attention to a *Career Builder Survey* which found that seventy-one per cent of employers valued EQ over IQ during the Fourth Industrial Revolution.[16] We are now past this date and, in many industries, their predictions have materialised.

Seeing IQ and EQ as opposing competencies is unhelpful because both work simultaneously. EQ is vital in order to *apply* IQ effectively.

Human beings are sometimes referred to as *Homo Sapiens* (the 'thinking species'). We have minds that are not only rational, operating deliberately and processing shades of nuance, but also emotional, operating intuitively and processing in

---

[14] Daniel Goleman, *Emotional Intelligence: Why it can matter more that IQ* (London: Bloomsbury Publishing), 1996.

[15] Available at: https://www.weforum.org/reports/the-future-of-jobs

[16] The Fourth Industrial Revolution refers to a digital revolution beginning around the year 2000, bringing with it growth in the speed and scope of storing, sharing and using data. The use of AI (Artificial Intelligence) lies at the heart of this movement. [The previous three Industrial Revolutions were focussed around Coal (1765), Gas (1870) and Electronics/Nuclear (1969)].

black and white. *Both* are essential to our humanity and set us apart from the rest of the animal kingdom.

In order to lead well we must learn to develop a healthy relationship with our own emotions and the emotions of others. Rather than suppressing emotions, we need to interpret and express them intelligently. Let's look at this more closely.

The word *emotion* comes from two Latin words: *motus* (movement) and *e* (away from) and carries the idea of movement away from a static position. Emotions are impulses causing us to act. These emotion impulses are usually manifested in specific psychological and physiological reactions, moving us away from our more settled state.

Here are some examples:

> *Anger* – heart rate increases as adrenalin readies the body to fight
>
> *Fear* – face grows pale as blood is shunted away to legs in readiness to flee danger
>
> *Happiness* – activity increases in the part of the brain that inhibits negative feelings
>
> *Surprise* – eyebrows lift to take in a larger visual sweep
>
> *Disgust* – nose wrinkles as a way of blocking obnoxious smells

The above effects often cause us to react on impulse alone. A well-developed emotional intelligence, on the other hand, enables a person to understand their own emotions and those of other people without feeling compelled to respond to impulses. Staying calm under pressure and learning to listen and co-operate effectively will help us keep these impulses in check. These abilities lie at the heart of emotional intelligence.

The American psychologist Howard Gardner published an influential book in 1983 called *Frames of Mind.* He differentiated between *intra*-personal intelligences (understanding self = self-awareness) and *inter*-personal intelligences (understanding others = empathy). This self-awareness and empathy prevents smart people being stupid!

To return to the illustration at the start, Lucy had an amazing IQ, meaning she was deemed to be a genius. Yet she lacked EQ – she struggled to read social situations and lacked self-control. If we are seeking to grow as a leader, we must not leave our emotional development to chance, but instead seek to develop our EQ as much as our other skills. Indeed, it is our EQ that is most likely to have the greatest bearing on our relationships with others.

Nudges

✐ Try to define *Emotional Intelligence* in a simple sentence.

✐ Are you aware of being a leader who can be "smart but stupid"?

✐ How self-aware do you think you are on a scale of 1-10? What could you do to push this number further to the right? (If you aren't sure, the following chapters will give you some ideas.)

CHAPTER 18

CURIOUS QUESTIONS – THE POWER OF OBSERVATION, LISTENING AND QUESTIONING

If you have ever spent long in the presence of a small child, you will know the feeling of being constantly bombarded with questions. Although it can be irritating, if we can learn to see past this and observe what is going on, there is much we can learn from the posture of a child. Children are like sponges, soaking up as much information as they can in any given situation. This requires them to be great observers, great listeners and great questioners. When they don't understand something, they remain restless until their curiosity is satisfied.

If we want to be effective leaders, there is a sense in which we ought to adopt this same approach. We cannot lead other people well if we do not understand them. Much can be learned simply through harnessing the power of observation, attentive listening and asking questions. Let's consider each in turn.

Effective leaders have cultivated the habit of being **great observers.**

Next time you are in a public place, find a comfortable bench or place to stand and spend twenty minutes simply observing people. Watch how they interact. Watch how they move and how fast. Watch their facial expressions and hand gestures. Look at the way they dress and carry themselves. What can you learn from other people simply through careful observation? This exercise will help form the *habit* of observation within you. This is something you can then carry into your own context with the people you know. Then try the same exercise when you are in the presence of a leader whom you respect. Intentionally reflect on what you observe. What is most notable to you? What impresses you? What challenges you? What surprises you? What can you learn from them? Which behaviours might you wish to emulate and which might you need to avoid? So many leadership habits are caught rather than taught; many of these through the simple discipline of observation.

We can also learn about other people through observation of what they have written. For many, this is the primary way they express themselves. What have they written? Why have they written it? What have they said? What have they not said? Never underestimate the power of observation. Perhaps we'd all do well to become leaders who are more child-like in this way?

Effective leaders have also set themselves the challenge of becoming **great listeners.**

Listening provides an opportunity to learn about others without needing to impose our own thoughts, our own impressions or our own agenda on them. So much of our listening is wrongly focussed on our response. True listening is about understanding. (We will think about this in greater depth in Chapter 26.)

Attentive listening is a means of passing power to the other person with the intention of learning rather than leading. By taking the posture of a learner, we empower another person to reveal more about themselves to us. This then becomes a vital means of getting in tune with the other person. Listening is one way of helping people become more comfortable in our presence, so that they share more openly and deeply about themselves. We often use the phrase 'paying attention'. This is quite apt when you think about it – attention is a valuable currency.

Whilst active listening will enable us to learn about someone else, we will also be passively teaching them about us. *How* we listen says a great deal about us as people.

Finally, effective leaders have trained themselves to **ask curious questions**.

Every person you could ever meet will know something that you don't. Curiosity helps us to listen without feeling the immediate need to respond. A curious listener seeks to find out more. The curious questioner asks: *Knowing what I now know, what more could I find out?* Asking this question is an incredibly effective tool for understanding other people more deeply. We will also be protected against making blind assumptions about another person.

Nudges

✐ Find someone you respect and consciously observe them. How do they lead themselves? How do they treat others? How do they respond to triumph and to failure? What do you learn through the questions they ask?

✐ What behaviour could you commit to that would help you become a more attentive listener?

✐ Can you think of an example of where you might benefit from relaxing your assumptions about something? How might growing a deeper curiosity help develop you as a leader?

CHAPTER 19

STANDING IN ANOTHER'S SHOES – COMMUNICATING FROM A PLACE OF UNDERSTANDING

The previous chapter explored the power of observation, listening and curiosity. Each can be harnessed as an effective tool for understanding other people. The next step to deeper understanding is to metaphorically seek to stand in their shoes. This typically involves asking three questions: Firstly, what do they see? Secondly, what do they feel? Thirdly, why does this matter to them?

Notice at the outset that the focus for all three questions is on the other person. The purpose of standing in another person's shoes is to understand them. We are not standing to comment or correct. We are choosing to *stand* in order to *understand*. This becomes particularly important when faced with a person with whom we might naturally clash. The whole of Part 5 is dedicated to handling conflict effectively. For now, however, let's address the three questions from above.

Firstly, standing in another person's shoes requires us to ask ourselves: *What do they see?* We will need to intentionally shift position in order to gain this different perspective. We can learn to see what they see either by asking them (and then of course listening carefully!) or simply through trying to imagine standing where they are standing. If you are facing a situation of conflict, ask yourself what it might be like to be facing you. Yes, that other person causes *you* frustration. But if the positions were reversed, you might see how you cause *them* frustration! If we can learn to see at least in part what others see, our communication will begin to come from a place of greater understanding.

Secondly, standing in another person's shoes requires us to ask ourselves: *What do they feel?* Feelings are essential to understand because they are one of the primary drivers for how we communicate. Appreciating another person's feelings is about displaying empathy[17], showing a concern for the person and not just for their output. Similarly, compassion is one of the gentlest skills a leader can exemplify but is ironically one of the strongest. If we can understand at least in part how another person feels, it can help shape what, how and when we communicate. Appreciating another person's feelings can also help prepare us for likely reactions and prevent unnecessary stress. I was interested to read a

---

[17] Brené Brown, *Dare to Lead* (London: Vermillion, 2018). Brené Brown is one of the most helpful writers on the subject of empathy and her bestselling book, *Dare to Lead*, is a great place to start. She has also contributed a number of useful *YouTube* videos on the subject. (Search: *Brené Brown Empathy*).

recent reflection by Jacinda Ardern, Prime Minister of New Zealand. She said this: *"One of the criticisms I've faced over the years is that I'm not aggressive enough or assertive enough, or maybe somehow, because I'm empathetic, I'm weak. I totally rebel against that. I refuse to believe that you cannot be both compassionate and strong."*[18]

Thirdly, standing in another person's shoes requires us to ask ourselves: *Why does this matter to them?* What a person values is an incredibly powerful driver of their behaviours. Understanding *what* matters to someone is the easy part. More difficult, but far more important, is understanding *why* it matters. Understanding 'why?' can be one way of determining the motivations that lie beneath actions. Understanding 'why?' can be a vital means of shedding much needed light in a challenging exchange that is otherwise only full of heat. Understanding 'why?' can help us deal with the disappointment of being let down.

If we want to be leaders who communicate effectively, we need to understand other people. So next time you are faced with a challenging situation, stop and ask yourself the three vital questions about the other person: What do they see? What do they feel? Why does this matter to them? You'll be a better leader for it.

---

[18] Posted in a Tweet by *The Women's Organisation*, April 19th 2020, 9am.

Nudges

✐ What do you think is a trait in you that has the greatest potential to cause other people frustration?

✐ Re-read Jacinda Arden's comment at the end of point 2 in this chapter. Do you agree or disagree? Where have you seen her attitude displayed in someone else?

✐ Which of the three questions in this chapter (*What do they see? What do they feel? Why do they feel it*) would you like to commit to asking more regularly to help you stand in another person's shoes?

CHAPTER 20

EVERYONE IS NORMAL UNTIL YOU GET TO KNOW THEM – DEVELOPING LEADERSHIP PATIENCE

Working with other people can be wonderful. Yet there is so often a hitch. People can be weird!

This may not be a conclusion we would reach initially. Indeed, to state this probably says more about our own issues than theirs! What is true, however, is that there is more to people than at first we see. Often, people who first come across as 'normal', soon show a different side when we get to know them.

We are complex beings and, as we saw in Part 1, we all have a back story. For good or for ill, these back stories complicate the process of understanding other people. As a result, relationships often induce what could be termed the *Porcupine Dilemma*: we need each other but how do we get close without hurting one another?

A foundational skill for understanding other people is developing leadership patience. Here are three reasons why.

Firstly, patience really enables us to appreciate the other person's story.

Both to hear their story and to appreciate it takes time. When we fail to listen carefully as leaders and assume we know a person when in reality we don't, we will have grossly failed to understand their story. Ironically, a person's story is arguably *the* primary determiner for the person they are today. If we miss their story, we are likely to miss valuable insights that will help us truly understand them.

Secondly, patience provides much needed perspective.

Patience can take us from a place of feeling *"I'm the only one around here who's normal,"* to a place of appreciating differences and, in time, celebrating them. Perspective is a vital tool for connection, helping us build deeper bonds with those who are similar to us and firmer bridges with those who are different.

Thirdly, the perspective that patience breeds also helps us approach conflict in a healthier manner.

When motivated by the desire to serve the other person, conflict can be a way to get under the surface and understand that person more deeply. Less experienced leaders can feel obliged to take on every challenge and 'sort' every conflict. Although this may be propelled by an admirable zeal, experience tells us that this is neither possible nor wise. Not every challenge has to be our challenge.

Learning to be patient helps us to reflect on our own attitudes before we seek to address the attitudes of others. Patience helps us pause and question our motives. All of this will help us to relate in a more life-giving way to other people, enabling us to move towards truly getting to know them. When we pose as a potential threat (either intentionally or unintentionally), the other person can raise their guard. By contrast, patience conveys gentleness and peaceability.

You may feel that the person in front of you is normal until you get to know them. The chances are they feel the same way towards you! The most effective leaders accept this and take positive steps to overcome it.

Nudges

✏ Can you think of a person whom you could work harder at building bridges with? What might this look like in practise?

✏ When you have made the right decision but in hindsight, realised it was made at the wrong time? What impact did this have on the responses of others, which in turn impacted your view of them?

✏ Being honest, who do you know whom you wrote off when you first met them, but now see much more positively?

CHAPTER 21

AUTHENTICITY AND VULNERABILITY – THE POWER OF BEING REAL

The subjects of the previous two chapters (understanding and patience) are vital ingredients for building relationships with other people. This helps them to lower their guard and become more real with us, thus opening the door to deeper authenticity and vulnerability. By displaying these traits ourselves, we will be able to draw them out in others.

The word *authentic* has become a bit of a buzz word in leadership conversations and is in danger of being overused. At the time of writing, an Amazon search revealed well over ten thousand books with this as the subject. So, what do we actually mean when we call one another towards greater authenticity?

Authenticity is in many ways about presence: living in the moment with conviction and confidence and staying true to yourself. The opposite is falsehood or being a clone of another. Authenticity involves being genuine in representing one's true self. At its simplest, authenticity is about being *real*.

Beware, however, of an overly simplistic understanding as this can limit your growth and impact as a leader by using the concept as an excuse for only ever sticking with what is comfortable. Authenticity does not equate to a person resisting change, as if they are a static reality.

The most effective leaders are able to develop what could be termed an *adaptive authenticity*. This is not about faking it. Instead, it is about figuring out what is the best way to relate to another person in the specific circumstance and then flexing in response. Our core personalities may not change a great deal but our behaviours certainly can. This social agility does not have to undermine authenticity. Authenticity is only undermined when our values become compromised and we behave in a way that is contrary to these values.

By displaying authenticity as leaders, we will foster trust which, in turn, will help draw authenticity out of others. We will not need to hide our imperfections, nor will we feel a constant pressure to impress. Authenticity gives us permission to be who we are and behave in a way that respects ourselves, whilst also respecting others. This, however, takes vulnerability.

Vulnerability involves a willingness to let go of who we think we *ought* to be, in order to be who we truly *are*. Genuine relationships are fuelled by connection. Vulnerability is a means of declaring to ourselves and to others, "*I am enough as I am,*" thereby establishing the connection on the basis of what is true. There is of course a risk that we will not be accepted. But why seek acceptance for something that is not the real us?

In many teams and organisations, being vulnerable is sadly frowned upon and wrongly equated to being a liability. Perhaps this is because we can be too quick to caricature vulnerability as a means of pathetically displaying our weaknesses in a *'woe is me'* kind of way. By contrast, true vulnerability takes great courage as it involves displaying compassion towards ourselves. Rather than constantly feeling inadequate, we are set free from our own expectation to be always on top of everything. In turn, we are enabled to display compassion towards other people. When people do not feel scrutinised by us, they are less likely to suffer from endless self-scrutiny themselves. Relationally, both sides feel freer to then be more real with one another.

Whilst it is understandable why we often choose to wear metaphorical armour to protect ourselves, this armour makes us relationally impenetrable and hampers genuine connection. Who would you most like to follow? The leader who always seems to have it all together or the leader who is real?

Nudges

As you consider the degree of authenticity that you display in your leadership, how consistent do you feel you are between your public life (what others see) and your private life (who you are when no-one is looking)?

✎   What are some of the factors that can drive you either to hide your imperfections or try to impress others? What impact does this have on the way you relate to yourself? To others?

✎   As you consider the issue of vulnerability, how compassionate do you think you are towards yourself? What benefit could it have on your relationships if you continued to develop in this area?

CHAPTER 22

BLINDED BY OTHERNESS - OVERCOMING UNCONSCIOUS BIAS

When it comes to understanding other people, it is easy to become blinded by their otherness. A natural unfamiliarity comes with those who are different from us. Rather than seeing this difference as an opportunity to grow and learn, we can end up becoming biased towards some people at the expense of others. Much of our bias is unconscious.

Unconscious biases are the attitudes or stereotypes that affect our views, our actions and our decision-making. Unconscious bias makes us predisposed to one person or group, over and above another. This leads unintentionally to categorising people. The power of unconscious bias lies in its subtlety, meaning most people are unaware of their own bias. Ask most people if they think they are biased and they will claim not to be. For those who can admit to their biases, few are able to see how deep they actually run.

The most obvious unconscious biases are racial, sexual, social or religious. There are also a number of other more subtle biases worth noting.

The illusion of inevitability - The tendency to make decisions based purely on the basis of previous outcomes.

Halo affect – The tendency to admire indiscriminately every action of a person on the basis of a positive first impression.

Affinity bias – Responding more favourably to people who are similar to us in terms of culture, personality, interests and beliefs.

Confirmation bias – Unconsciously seeking out evidence to confirm initial perceptions whilst simultaneously ignoring evidence to the contrary.

Information framing – The use of excess, inadequate or inaccurate information can alter how we 'frame' a situation. This can powerfully influence how decisions are made and how we view other people.

Fear and peer pressure – Allowing the desire for harmony and conformity to distort more objective assessments of an environment or a person. Perhaps this plays out in running with an idea even when you disagree, for fear of backlash from a strong character or from someone whose opinion you value too much.

Decision preference – Responding more favourably to certain people based on our preferred way of making decisions. Some people are wired to make decisions based on a preference for objective reasoning and impersonal facts. Others are wired to make decisions based on empathy and personal concerns. The former might incline you to make value judgments based on the logic of an argument, but blind you to EQ cues (remember Chapter 17?). The latter might incline you to make value judgements based on how a person makes you feel, but blind you to the merits of their argument.

Self-awareness helps us become more aware of other people, appreciating them for their merits and not using difference as a reason to distance ourselves from them. Effective leadership intentionally and regularly seeks to overcome the natural blindness that can affect us all. This enables us to overcome unconscious biases and get to know others with a more heart-felt integrity.

Nudges

✎ Can you think of where you might naturally exhibit unconscious bias in your leadership? What impact might this have on people's trust in you? What practical steps could you take to overcome these tendencies?

✎ Have you ever experienced behaviours towards you that would suggest unconscious bias in another person? What was the impact?

✎ What could you do to help other people recognise and act against their own biases?

CHAPTER 23

TRANSACTIONAL V TRANSFORMATIONAL - DEEPLY CARING ABOUT OTHERS

There are two principal ways to relate to another person: transactional and transformational.

We can define transactional relationships are those that are consciously or subconsciously focussed on ourselves. As a result, they end up being relationships of transaction, focussed on what we can gain from the other person. *How can they give me the information I need so that I can get on with my job? How can I persuade them to agree with me so that we can move on? How can I avoid unnecessary communication with this difficult person?* Transactional relationships are often so focussed on the task that the other person comes a firm second. Transactional relationships short-change both parties as vital opportunities for growth are inevitably missed.

Transformational relationships on the other hand are primarily focussed on the other person. They are motivated by a desire to serve, caring for the other person's wellbeing and aiding their development. The focus shifts from our own agenda and success towards championing others. Done well, the primary focus is on the other person, without losing the necessary task element. Transformational relationships are mutual.

Remember that people are complex. What motivates one person may not necessarily motivate another. As you reflect on the way you relate to others and seek to motivate them, where does your focus most naturally lie?

Below are a few observations of why so many well-intended relationships quickly become transactional:

- Transactional relationships take less time and energy (so are easier)
- Tiredness and stress can cause us to overfocus on the task and neglect the personal element.
- We might find it easy to pick up bad habits from those around us.
- Deeply caring for others is often unseen and unre-warded, and so sadly undervalued.

What might you add to this list?

Now consider some of the benefits of transformational relationships:

- They help build deeper trust and respect.
- They foster a life-giving team culture.
- They deepen emotional awareness and empathy.
- They help grow other people's self-awareness and leadership depth.

- They model a way of relating that we would like to receive ourselves.
- They reduce stress in team members, leading to longer-term productivity and fulfilment. *

* This is often called *discretionary effort*. It describes a level of effort people could give, over and above what they are currently giving. Discretionary effort is often motivated by having a clear sense of purpose and being valued. Most people will care more about their work if they feel cared for as people. This is why team culture is just as important as team task.

Specific contexts will shape what caring for another person could look like. Rather like a golf player who carries a range of clubs in her bag, leaders need to carry different approaches to caring and learn to select the right one for each occasion. Caring is about deeply valuing others for the unique contribution they can bring and actively seeking to help them make this contribution.

As you build relationships and your internal database of the most effective ways to relate to others enlarges, you will become like a skilled golfer: the same player but regularly changing your club.

Deeply caring for others is often an undervalued behaviour. Building a reputation as one who really cares will help you build deep relational capital with others and is always a valuable investment. You never know when *you* might need caring for.

Nudges

✐ Where are you in danger of relating to others trans-
actionally as opposed to transformationally? What
could you do to avoid this tendency?

✐ Try to think of an example where you have been
deeply cared for by another person. How has this
increased the discretionary effort you have been prepared to expend yourself?

✐ What are some of the 'clubs' you carry around that
help you best care for others? In what situations do
you need to play a gentle chip, nudging a person in
a particular direction? When might you need to play
a harder drive? When do you need to lay down your
clubs and study the course a little longer, perhaps listening rather than responding?

CHAPTER 24

LEARNING FROM YOUR NEMESIS – THE GIFT OF OTHER PEOPLE

Think for a moment of a person you find it particularly difficult to relate to. What is it about them and their behaviour that most challenges you? Most leaders have at least one 'thorn in their flesh'! Now reflect on the times when their behaviour has brought out the worst in you. Why has been the impact?

Think what a difference it would make if you could learn to view this person (let's call them your *nemesis*) as a gift as opposed to a problem. Difficult people will help develop more self-control and self-awareness than easy people. Difficult people can help develop your character and your ability to lead other challenging people.

What might need to change in your perspective in order to turn your nemesis into a very real gift? Below are four suggestions:

Difference: a threat or an opportunity?

Every person you meet has a different character and temperament with different attitudes and behaviours, and different ways of processing information and communicating. Do you see this difference as a threat or an opportunity? The way you answer this will go a long way towards explaining how you approach complex and challenging relationships. Whilst difference presents obvious challenge, it also presents the opportunity for us to grow and develop. Handling difference also presents us with opportunity to help the other person grow.

Exposing the root

Often when we engage in a challenging relationship, the first thing we absorb is the way this person makes us feel. This feeling can often trigger an emotional reaction that is not always helpful. If we learn to pause first and seek to discern underlying issues, our response may be more helpful. We can learn to expose the root rather than just responding to the fruit.

For example, when a team member is short with us and overly critical, we might easily respond emotionally out of a feeling of *"that is unfair, and I'd better make it known"*. Yet, if we could see below the surface, we might find that their critical words are only a symptom of a deeper issue – perhaps a recent bereavement or hidden stress that we know nothing about. Reflecting on the possible root of a person's behaviour before reacting *to* the behaviour is a subtle and powerful skill for a leader to develop. Understanding helps us respond rather than react. There is a difference.

The respect boomerang

We saw in the previous chapter the importance of deeply caring for others. This involves focussing on transformational relationships as opposed to transactional ones. Respecting others, particularly our nemesis, is a huge part of caring for others. It is a truism that what goes around, comes around. Showing respect to others, especially to those we find difficult, may well motivate them to respect you when they are finding you difficult. Throw the respect boomerang out and you are far more likely to get it back.

Remember you are someone else's nemesis!

Reflecting on your experiences with your nemesis can become a helpful tool for your self-understanding. Just as person X may be your nemesis, so you may be person Y's nemesis. We should remember that it is foolish always to assume that the problem lies with other people. Consider what behaviours you exhibit that might be a challenge to other people. Are you open to exploring ideas other than your own? When you hear an opinion other than your own, what do you really say to yourself subconsciously? (Be honest!)

We have much to learn from those we find challenging. This learning starts when we accept them as a gift for our growth rather than a problem to avoid.

Nudges

🖊 Humility (see Chapter 10) is vital when rubbing up against other people who see things differently from us. How might this thought help you and challenge you as a leader?

🖊 Think back to the last difficult meeting you were in. Consider how the topics in the last seven chapters might have helped you approach the people in that meeting differently.

🖊 How might the recognition that you will be someone else's nemesis impact the way you view your own nemesis?

PART 4

COMMUNICATING EFFECTIVELY

"The single biggest problem in communication is the illusion that it has taken place."

George Bernard Shaw
Irish playwright and political activist

"The audience does not need to tune themselves to you—you need to tune your message to them. Skilled presenting requires you to understand their hearts and minds and create a message to resonate with what's already there."

Nancy Duarte
Communications Specialist and Author of *Resonate*

In a world full of noise and endless distraction, the ability to be heard and understood is a key skill of any leader. There is all the difference in the world between communication and *effective* communication. Effective communication is all about connection and it is through connection that we are able to meaningfully influence people. Effective communication is an art, not a science. So often it is the small things that make the biggest difference.

CHAPTER 25

LIVING ON THE OTHER SIDE OF YOU – BEING GREAT TO TALK TO

What are you like to talk to?

Perhaps this is not a question we've asked ourselves before. We certainly know what other people are like to talk to! But what about ourselves? One of the marks of great leadership is being brilliant to talk to. These kind of leaders understand who they are (Part 1) and have a strong understanding of who others are (Part 2). This enables them to connect with people quickly and with empathy which in turn builds meaningful relationships that are life-giving.

If we want to become better to talk to, it is worth considering how we build attention, connection and affection. Let's consider each in turn.

Attention

When you are in conversation with someone, do they have your full attention? Are you fully present and in the moment, not just physically being there but choosing to be emotionally present as well? Giving others our undivided attention is not only a way of showing respect but also a means of having a more enjoyable and profitable conversation. Giving someone our attention is an intentional way of displaying that this person (whether simply a passing acquaintance or someone with whom we have an established relationship) is important and valued.

You don't have to be an egotist to appreciate people giving you attention. Attention ought to be a common courtesy and something that makes a huge difference to conversation, especially in a hurried world where attention spans are ever-shortening. Attentive listening is a key skill in leadership (we will look at this in more detail in our next chapter). Consider asking yourself *who the spotlight is on* when you are in conversation. Brilliant conversationalists don't make it all about themselves!

Connection

A lot of the words we speak fail to have an impact because they never land. This is often because the important work of bridging gaps has not taken place. Connection is a vital skill needed if we are to become brilliant to talk to. Connection begins by showing a genuine respect for and interest in another person. Connection helps build relational capital and is often a foundation to fall back on in situations of conflict. Connection enables us to share ourselves with others with greater authenticity and vulnerability.

Whilst much conversation is necessarily spontaneous, there are times when more careful thought is required as to the best way to handle issues and the people concerned. Careful preparation can help maximise connection.

We must also not forget that two people don't have to be in agreement to experience connection. They just have to know that the other person cares. Body language is a key player in this dynamic. The way we carry ourselves, the use of our physical presence, facial expressions and hand gestures each play a role in establishing and maintaining connection. What do you already do well? Where is there room for growth? Working hard to establish meaningful connection is the second step to becoming brilliant to talk to.

Affection

Affection in this context refers not to liking or loving another person but about following that person's affections in conversations: what excites them? moves them? motivates them? saddens them? Following the other person's affections is what helps them leave the conversation feeling valued. Affection is not a display of sympathy (*"I know how you feel"*) but a display of empathy (*"I feel for how you feel"*).

Whilst it is true that people may not leave a conversation remembering everything you said, they will always remember how you made them feel.

Nudges

- Being brilliant to talk to involves attention, connection and affection. What do you already do well? Where is there room for growth?

- What word or phrase would you use to describe how a person might typically feel after spending an hour with you?

- How could you alter your behaviour so that you will become better to talk to?

CHAPTER 26

THE MISSING HALF OF COMMUNICATION - BEING A LEADER WHO LISTENS

The world has become a very noisy place, making it hard to listen to ourselves, let alone others! We tend to operate at such a fast pace that much of our listening becomes fragmented and hurried. The art of true conversation is sadly being replaced with personal broadcasting. Most people prefer to speak than to listen, which turns many conversations into little more than intersecting monologues.

The noise of the outside world and noise in our own lives makes it hard to truly listen. Were this trajectory to continue, the world would become a very scary world indeed. Sadly, this is the world many of us already experience, and dare I say it, may even contribute to.

In 2012 Google launched *Project Aristotle*[19] with the aim of improving relationships across the global enterprise. One of

---

[19] Cited in: Charles Duhigg. "What Google Learned From Its Quest to Build the Perfect Team". *New York Times Magazine*, February 25th, 2016.

the key questions employees were asked was, *"What makes a great team?"* One hundred and eighty teams were interviewed across Google over a three-year period. Five major outcomes were discerned, one of which was the value of being listened to through having a voice in the organisation.

Listening is without doubt the missing half of communication, absolutely necessary but often overlooked.[20] Listening is a primary way of showing respect and affirming the value of another person's contributions. Below are three reflections aimed at helping us all improve our listening skills.

Listening to respond or listening to understand?

Do you typically listen to respond or listen to understand? The former kills true conversation, the latter fosters meaningful dialogue. One way to diagnose this in yourself is to think about the difference between a *Shift Response* and a *Support Response*.

---

[20] I would recommend the following four resources if you want to commit to becoming a better listener:

Kate Murphy, *You're Not Listening: What You're Missing and Why it Matters* (London: Harville Secker, 2020).

Zack Zenger and Joseph Folkman. "What Great Listeners Actually Do". *Harvard Business Review*, July 2016. Available at: hbr.org/2016/07/what-great-listeners-actually-do.   Accessed   17th December 2020.

Susan Cain, *Quiet: The Power of Introverts in a World That Can't Stop Talking* (London: Penguin, 2013).

William Ury. "The Power of Listening" *TEDxSanDiego*, January 2015. Available at: www.youtube.com/watch?v=saXfavo1OQo . Accessed 24th October 2020.

Suppose a teammate says to you in conversation: *"My dog escaped last week and it took three days to find her.* How would you naturally respond to this?

An example of a Shift Response would be: *"Our dog is always digging under the fence. We don't let him out unless she's on a leash."* Notice how the listener shifts the focus from the one talking to themselves.

By way of contrast, an example of a Support Response might be: *"Oh no. Where did you finally find her?"* Notice how the listener's focus here is on understanding and expressing a curiosity to find out more. By responding with a question, they are supporting what has been said and keeping the focus on the one speaking.

A second example: *"I watched this really good documentary about robots last night."* Shift Response: *"I'm not big into documentaries. I'm more of an action film kind of guy."* Support Response: *"Robots?! That sounds cool. What were you learning?"*

Leaders who listen become known for giving Support Responses rather than Shift Responses.

Conflicting communication styles

A second reflection involves thinking about the reality that every communication style has an opposite. One particular style of communicating may connect with this group of people but grate on that group. Why? The answer is that every person or group tends to be wired towards a favoured communication style. Here are some examples of opposing communication styles:

> Expressive vs Reflective
>
> Rational vs Emotional

Animated vs Detached

Direct vs Diplomatic

Detailed vs Big picture

Earnest vs Restrained

For each one, try to establish which is most characteristic of the way you prefer to communicate. Then consider one practical thing you could consciously do to communicate in a more life-giving way in the opposing example. (We will consider this in greater detail in the next chapter.)

Listening with a third ear

A third reflection is to consider what some people call *listening with a third ear*. This involves not just paying attention to the words spoken, but also learning to gather non-verbal cues such as body language, facial expressions and tone. Doing these things regularly will help develop empathy and connection and significantly aid our development as leaders who listen.

Nudges

✐ Write down the first line of an imaginary conversation. Then try to write out some examples of a shift response and support response.

✐ Who do you know who is a brilliant listener? What impact does this have on your interactions?

✐ Try starting every conversation this week with a question. What do you notice?

CHAPTER 27

A RUBBER TONGUE - THE POWER OF FLEXING COMMUNICATION STYLE

We all have a preferred communication style, as the diagram below outlines. Which one best describes you? Which would you say comes second? Which style is least natural to you?

Logical	Direct
Questionning	Clear
Precise	Concise
Factual	Action focussed
Communication Styles	
Diplomatic	Emotional
Sincere	Personal
Courteous	Expressive
Gentle	Emotive

None of the above styles should be declared as being better or more suited to leadership. Each has its strengths. The skill of the leader involves the ability to read the situation or person in front of them and, in light of this, communicate most appropriately. Some people call this communicating with a *rubber tongue.* The ability to flex is a sign of the social agility of the leader, either focussing on one communication style, tempering or emphasising it as appropriate, or flexing towards another style.

In reality, all of our communication will be a blend of all four styles, although we are likely to gravitate towards one or two styles that most suit our temperament or what our circumstances demand of us. In general, the style diagonally opposite to your preferred style is likely to be the one you find hardest to flex towards and therefore will be the style that communicates *least* effectively with you.

Flexing our styles takes energy, which is why, when we are stressed, we will naturally revert to our preferred type. Each of the four styles above will have a few bad day behaviours associated with them, as shown below:

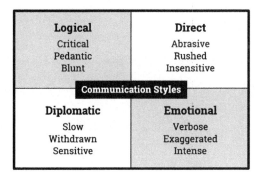

Logical	Direct
Critical	Abrasive
Pedantic	Rushed
Blunt	Insensitive

Communication Styles

Diplomatic	Emotional
Slow	Verbose
Withdrawn	Exaggerated
Sensitive	Intense

As you consider your leadership within the context you are currently in, how might the thoughts in this chapter enable you to display a greater versatility in your communication style? What difference might this make?

Nudges

✎ When have you experienced someone flexing their approach in order to best communicate with you? What was the impact?

✎ What is the impact on you when people communicate with you in each of the four styles outlined in this chapter?

✎ When adopting each of the four communication styles, which one requires you to flex the most? What difference might this make in some of your relationships if you learnt to adapt to this style more readily?

CHAPTER 28

MAKING EVERY WORD COUNT – COMMUNICATING WITH CLARITY

Have you ever noticed how some of the most influential leaders are those who speak the least, but when they do speak it has a real impact? Equally, have you ever noticed the distinctive power that comes when a leader communicates with crystal clarity? No waffle, no unnecessary repetition. Just simple, clear and engaging. To be able to communicate in this way is a real gift. Few people naturally have it, but we can all work harder to get better. Clarity is important as it enables our words to really count and have meaningful impact. Clarity is just as much about what you *don't* say as what you do say. Clarity is also important because of the positive influence it can have on overcoming fixed mindsets and implementing change.

Suppose for example you are a leader who is seeking to convey a new vision to the team you lead. You prepare carefully, deliver the vision, but go away demoralised because half the team unexpectedly showed resistance to your ideas. In such moments it is perfectly possible that what we see as resistance may in reality be a reaction to our own lack of clarity.

Below are five principles of communicating with clarity:

Know your Big Idea

Each time you communicate, try to be clear in your own mind exactly what you want to say. This principle becomes particularly important as your experience and knowledge pool grows. Learn to be selective and share only what is *most* helpful for the people in front of you. Try to make your big idea a single crisp sentence that is easily repeatable and therefore memorable.

Practise on a ten-year-old

Remember that simple does not mean simplistic. Complex ideas can be conveyed simply as long as the ideas are crystal clear in your own head. One way to test the clarity of something you need to explain is by practising on a ten-year-old. They will soon expose any unhelpful jargon, jumbled ideas or unnecessary complexity.

Adrian Burdon said this of the great English preacher and orator John Wesley:

> *"The simplicity of John Wesley's preaching was his glory. This simplicity had not been easily attained, but was the result of many years of effort … [He] read his sermons to an intelligent maid-servant who agreed to stop him every time he came to a word she did not understand. She shouted 'Stop, sir!' so often that Wesley became impatient. He schooled himself thereafter to express himself clearly and simply and was rewarded by the knowledge that the congregation could understand his message."[21]*

---

[21] Adrian Burdon. "The Preaching Service - The Glory of the Methodists". *Grove Liturgical Study*, 64, 1991, p.8.

Ditch the notes

Whilst this may make you feel desperately uncomfortable at first, committing to speaking without notes forces you to be clear in both what you say and also the order in which you say it. This is certainly a skill to develop, but over time you will find far more freedom to express yourself and communicate from your heart in an authentic way if you are not tied to a tight script. If necessary, have a cue card with a few buzzwords or pictures to trigger specific things you need to say.

Never miss an opportunity to shut up!

This is the principle of being clear and concise and not feeling the pressure to fill pauses with repetition or verbal dribble. After you have spoken, give people time to respond. Remember that some people process new information through discussion and others prefer to reflect in their own minds. Silence does not automatically convey disengagement. By listening carefully to (and observing) the response of your listeners, you will be in a better position to know if it is appropriate or not to speak again.

Watch and learn

Whether you lack confidence as a communicator of feel you're qualified to deliver a State of the Nation Address to millions, we all have room for growth. A great way to grow in communication clarity is to watch others who exemplify this skill. Listen to what they say, but also to what they do not say. Listen up for how they order ideas in their minds and then deliver them in memorable ways. If this is something you genuinely feel you do very well, you may be able to draw alongside someone else to help them improve.

Nudges

✎ Of the leaders you know, who communicates the most clearly? What do you think makes them so clear? What impact does it have?

✎ What might it look like for your leadership communication to became clearer? Clearer ideas? Clearer vision? Clearer presentation?

✎ How does the idea of speaking without notes make you feel? How might the concepts of clarity explained in this chapter help you to give it a go?

CHAPTER 29

A PICTURE PAINTS A THOUSAND WORDS – HELPING PEOPLE SEE WHAT YOU ARE SAYING

Much of the way that we ordinarily communicate ignores the fact that many people are visual learners. Words in themselves do not always connect. However, when we use words to paint pictures, the situation changes. Effective communicators help people to *see* what they are saying. This can be through spoken word, written text or even embodied action.

In their excellent book *Made to Stick*[22], Chip and Dan Heath ask why some messages stick and others do not. Using the acronym SUCCES, they outline six characteristics of Sticky messages. Interestingly, each one in a different way helps people to see what you are saying.

---

[22] Chip Heath and Dan Heath, *Made to Stick: Why some ideas take hold and others come unstuck* (London: Arrow, 2008).

Simple – Make relevant information interesting and ignore that which is irrelevant, even though it may be interesting. Simplicity enables a message to hit and stick with a core idea. Anyone can make simple things complicated. It is a real skill to make complicated things simple.

Unexpected – Look to surprise and force listeners to ask questions, rather than just absorb information. Create suspense and curiosity by exposing knowledge gaps.

Concrete – Use illustrations that appeal to familiarity and are therefore memorable.

Credible – Use detail to enhance credibility. These might be facts, observations or anecdotes.

Emotional – Make associations with things that people already care about. Try to pre-empt their *"so what?"* responses and answer them. Appeal to imagination. Use humour where appropriate.

Story – Build connection and draw people in by appealing to the power of story. Stories capture imagination and are a great way of connecting with both heart and mind. (We will look at this in more detail in our next chapter.)

Think back to the last important message you communicated. How *sticky* was it? Which of the above characteristics could you have employed to better effect? Helping people see what you are saying is particularly important when trying to persuade them about a new idea or vision. Just because an idea is clear in your mind doesn't automatically mean it will be clear in theirs.

Have a look back at Chapter 27: A Rubber Tongue - *The Power of Flexing Communication Style.* For each of the four communication styles that are explained there, try to consider how the six characteristics of *sticky* messages from this chapter could apply. You may find the following grid a helpful way of ordering your thoughts.

Communication Style (Chapter 27)	'Sticky' Characteristic (this chapter)					
	SIMPLE	UNEXPECTED	CONCRETE	CREDIBLE	EMOTIONAL	STORY
LOGICAL						
DIRECT						
EMOTIONAL						
DIPLOMATIC						

Nudges

✎ How effective do you think you are at helping people *see* what you are saying?

✎ Pay attention to Radio adverts over the next month or so. Notice how effective they are at painting pictures in our minds.

✎ Do you feel you are most effective as a leader by using spoken words, written prose or embodied action? How could you play to these strengths and work on the areas where you are weaker?

CHAPTER 30

ONCE UPON A TIME - HARNESSING THE POWER OF STORY

Stories have been used for thousands of years as a medium for cultures to pass on their morals, laws and tales of conquest. Stories were a means of connecting with the masses, especially in the days when much of the average population was illiterate. Most stories fit one of six paradigms: Overcoming the Enemy, Rebirth and Renewal, Quest and Adventure, Journey and Return, Rags to Riches, Tragedy and Comedy. Each of these paradigms appeals to humanity because of the connection to our own experiences.

Stories are a powerful means of transcending cultures and geographical boundaries. They capture hearts and minds and are memorable and therefore repeatable. One of the reasons stories appeal to us so much is because they demonstrate transformation. By observing change in other people, we can be encouraged to notice and commit to change in our own lives.

Stories are an incredibly powerful tool in the leader's armoury and are often underused. To tell a good story, you just need to remember your vowels - A.E.I.O.U.[23]

A – Attention

The first moments of any story are amongst the most powerful. These are the moments that grab our attention and cause us to focus in. Whenever you are communicating something important as a leader, it is vital you work hard to get your hearers' attention. Whilst you will have been living and breathing your ideas and are completely focussed on them, the point at which you first engage your hearers will be a point where their minds are likely to be elsewhere. What can you do to help them dial in to what you need to communicate? Without gaining their attention, the rest of your story is likely to become lost. You know this is true because when you talk to a dull person, it doesn't take much for you to switch off. Similarly, you rarely persevere beyond the first couple of pages of a book if it has failed to grab your attention. (The fact that you have reached this point in this book I hope is a good sign!)

E – Empathy

Empathy is a crucial part of telling a story, helping you demonstrate to another person that you understand them. It is a means of standing in their shoes and feeling what they feel. Empathy helps people feel that you are not talking *at* them and are instead communicating *with* them. Take for example Martin Luther King Junior's famous speech. He

---

[23] I am grateful to Richard Garnett and Russell Boulter for first sharing this idea with me at a communications workshop.

built empathy by appealing to the hearts of his listeners. His speech did not begin, "*I have a plan*", but, "*I have a dream*", capturing people's imagination and inviting them to share his dream.

I – Insight

In a world bursting with information, insight helps your message stand out from the crowd. Information produces noise; insight produces clarity. Providing key insights will help your message stand out. The temptation to provide an overload of information will water down your message and drown out the big idea you are seeking to convey. What does the person in front of you *most* need to hear *at this time?* Everything else can be ignored or wait for another time. Delivering key messages with insight is as much about what you *don't* say as what you do say. Think about serving a steak rather than the whole cow!

O – Options

Powerful communication moves from providing insights to handing the baton over to the hearer and asking for a response. Providing options forces your listeners to engage and make a decision. One effective way of doing this is to ask '*What if I do?*' vs '*What if I don't?*' questions. These questions force people to consider what is at stake.

U - Over you U!

Having provided options, be clear on what the action button is. What are you calling people to do? To feel? To say? To consider? Most people will not naturally take action unless they are called to do so. The best communicators are masters at handing over responsibility so that their hearers learn to be the solution to their own problem. In this way, the hearers become the heroes in the story, increasing their engagement and sense of achievement.

What could all of the above look like in practice? Imagine you are seeking to help your team overcome a seemingly insurmountable problem. How could you harness the power of story and 'make use of your vowels' to best help them? If it were me, I could link the team's apprehension to a time when I was a little boy, standing at the bottom of a huge mountain, overwhelmed by the prospect of trying to walk up it with my dad. I could re-tell the story, carefully working through 'my vowels' and then connect the story to the situation my team was faced with in that moment. The inspiration of a little boy facing up to a challenge, persevering through multiple moments of "*I can't do this*" and eventually standing on top of the mountain – this could be the sort of story that unlocks the fears in my own team and gives them the necessary motivation not to give up themselves.

What story could you tell?

Nudges

🖊 What memorable story has most captured your imagination? How has it inspired you?

🖊 As you reflect on the A.I.E.O.U above, which do you feel you could most intentionally develop?

🖊 Think of a situation coming up where you may have to persuade people to follow you. How could you turn this into a compelling story that gives a clear call to action?

CHAPTER 31

UNLOCKING DOORS – BEING PERSUASIVE WITHOUT BEING PUSHY

Effective leaders are influencers. They have the ability to open locked doors and persuade people to follow them or adopt particular ideas. This does not mean the idea has to have come from the leader. (In order to maximise empowerment, it is often best that they don't.) There will be times though when the team looks to you to make a call. In these moments, the art of persuasion is hugely important.

The diagram below illustrates that when a normal distribution of people are presented with a new idea, their likely responses will include Innovators, Early Adopters, Early Majority, Late Majority, Late Adopters and Laggards. Innovators and Early Adopters rarely need persuading and the Early Majority normally move with some persuasion. Late Adopters often need a lot of persuasion and Laggards tend never to be persuaded.

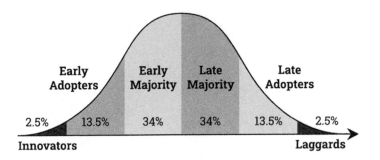

As you look at this diagram, which group do you think is best suited to persuade the Late Majority and Late Adopters to move to the left? The answer, perhaps surprisingly, is *not* the Innovators or Early Adopters. Their role is to persuade the Early Majority, who in turn can influence the groups behind. This cascading persuasion-pull then becomes very effective.

As you think about situations where you need to be persuasive, consider the five principles laid out below. If you were to adopt one, which would help you the most?

Camera Angle

Persuasion will look very different depending on who is in front of you. It is helpful to look at what you are seeking to communicate from different camera angles or perspectives. Sometimes the angle from which you attack an issue becomes all-important.

The Three 'Musketeers': Ethos, Pathos and Logos

Ethos is ethical persuasion, appealing to a person's character. Ethos shows that you value what they value. Pathos is imaginative persuasion, appealing to a person's emotions. Pathos involves the use of empathy and a sense of feeling what the other person feels. Logos is evidential persuasion, appealing to a person's reason. Logos is logical and underpinned by facts as a means of displaying that you understand what the other person is thinking.

Paint a compelling picture

Remember to help people to *see* what you are saying rather than just saying it. (Remember Chapter 29?)

Set up, don't sell

The best salespeople are those who have learned the art of asking penetrating questions that set the buyer up to see that they have a need and must therefore act to fulfil this need. Being pushy in sales rarely works these days unless you're a door-to-door salesman and people offer to pay you to go away! Robert Cialdini has written about an interesting concept which he calls *Pre-Suasion*:[24] focusing on what can be done to build relationships before a sales pitch or sharing a challenging vision. *Pre*-suasion is the work that enables our persuasion to be more effective. What might this look like for you in your context?

Timing

Knowing when to advance and when to wait is one of the great discernment tools for any leader. We will think about this more in the next chapter.

---

[24] Robert B. Cialdini, *Pre-Suasion: A Revolutionary Way to Influence and Persuade* (New York: Random House Business, 2016).

Cialdini's *Pre-Suasion* concept is also covered in his bestselling book, *Influence, The Psychology of Persuasion* (New York: HarperBus, 2007). A new and expanded edition is due for publication in May 2021.

Nudges

🖉 As you reflect on your own leadership and situations where you have had to persuade others about something, which has come most naturally, Ethos, Pathos or Logos? Where do you have most room for development?

🖉 Can you see why Part 2, *Understanding Others*, is so vital to effective communication? It is almost impossible to persuade people about a particular course of action until we first understand who they are and how they think.

🖉 Can you recall an occasion where you had a compelling vision and clear story, but the timing was wrong for putting it across? What have you learned from this?

CHAPTER 32

WHAT, WHY, HOW, WHEN? – THE SIGNIFICANCE OF TIMING

Often what matters most is not *what* is said or *why* it is said or even *how* it is said, as vital as all of these things are. The most significant element of what we say is often the *timing* of it. Below are four ideas to consider that could help you improve your communication timing.

Yes or No?

It takes great discernment to know when to hold back and observe and when to stand up and speak. Remember that nothing that has been said can be un-said. This means that saying the right thing at the wrong time is likely to be deemed the wrong thing. Conversely, opportunities to say something do not linger forever and it is easy to miss the boat if we waver too long. To discern whether your 'when' is a *now* or a *later* in any given moment, it is always worth pausing first and asking this question: *"Will this be the best thing for this person right now?"* If *"yes"*, go for it! If you are unsure, best to hold back. By asking ourselves this question, we shift the focus away from ourselves and what may be best for us. Instead, our focus moves to serving the other person.

Context

Appreciation of your context can help in the discernment process of optimal timing. Who are you speaking to? How well do you know them? Is this your first interaction or a repeated conversation? When dealing with sensitive issues, is this a time to be discreet or opt instead for maximum transparency? Asking such questions is particularly important when offering challenge. Sometimes this is best done in group settings. Other times one-to-one. Choosing an appropriate time, based on context, is essential.

Sleep on it

If you have a difficult conversation or big issue to discuss, the timing becomes even more important. The principle of 'sleep on it' has saved many leaders from making huge mistakes. What seems like a good idea towards the end of one day, may prove in the cold light of a new day to be an absolute no-go. This is particularly important given our regular use of instantaneous messaging via email, text and social media posts. These can all be great tools but can just as easily become terrible enemies. Try to get in the habit of saving drafts and returning to them the next morning.

A word in season

The power of encouragement as a leader must never be underestimated. Compassionate leaders know what it means to faithfully walk alongside someone as a fellow-traveller and from this place, speak a word in season with great power. This is not about making grand statements or offering soundbites of advice. Rather, it is so often about accurately judging where another person is at and choosing the right time to say the simple thing, that in the moment truly counts.

Which of the above challenges you the most? Which one of the ideas, if adopted, would make the biggest difference to your leadership? (We will cover these issues more in Part 5 as we consider how to handle conflict wisely.)

Nudges

✎ Try to think of a time when someone has spoken the right thing to you at the wrong time. What was the impact?

✎ *"There is a time to speak and a time to remain silent"* (Proverbs 15:23). Are you someone who naturally hangs back, waiting for a better moment to say something but soon realises the opportunity is lost? Or are you someone who naturally speaks up quickly but later regrets jumping in too fast? Understanding our natural tenancies can help prevent us from leaning towards them too heavily.

✎ The best leaders are encouragers. What practical things could you do to help yourself remember significant dates, times and events in order to encourage another person in a very timely way?

PART 5

HANDLING CONFLICT WISELY

"Never let your fears prevent you from doing what you know is right."

Aung San Suu Kyi
Burmese Politician and 1991
Nobel Peace Prize laureate

"Whenever you are in conflict with someone, there is one factor that can make the difference between damaging your relationship and deepening it. That factor is attitude."

William James
Father of American Psychology

Facing conflict as a leader is inevitable. It is quite normal to feel inadequate, particularly if you are newer to a leadership role or responsibility. It takes great courage and discernment to handle conflict in a way that brings life. In this section of this book we will look at some key principles to help you view conflict not as something to avoid, but rather as something that can enable you and other people to grow.

CHAPTER 33

R.E.S.P.E.C.T -
What do you owe the person
with whom you disagree?

Observing a recent political rivalry and election, I was shocked by the prevalence of condescension, biting accusation and a constant talking over one another in debates and rallies. Aggression and shouting louder than your opponent seemed to be the only means of getting heard. There was very little mutual respect and their handling of differences demonstrated a poor example of leadership to a watching world.

The good news, however, is that we can learn from poor examples as much as good ones, largely through personal resolve to act differently when placed in similar situations. One of the best questions we could ask ourselves each and every time we face potential conflict is this: *what do I owe the person with whom I disagree?*

So many of the choices we make can have a profoundly positive or negative impact on others. These choices are largely determined by the way we think about another person. Making the deliberate choice to respect another person is a fundamental means of having a positive impact. Respecting others does not necessarily mean we need to like or agree with them. Rather, respect is about remembering that the person with whom we may disagree is a person with a unique identity and inherent value. We must never reduce others to valueless targets for our frustration.

What might this look like? Let's consider a useful acronym: *R.E.S.P.E.C.T.* - Remember, Empathy, Sincerity, Patience, Equality, Courtesy, Truthfulness.

Remember

Pausing to *think* before we speak can help us remember who is in front of us. *What might it feel like for them to be on the opposite side of me? Do they need challenge or support? How might this conflict be an opportunity for us both to grow? What responsibility do I need to take to ensure this conflict ends up being life-giving?* Carefully thinking about the person in front of us can help us to respond appropriately.

Empathy

As we saw earlier in Chapters 17 and 19, empathy displays an understanding of the other person and a desire to stand in their shoes and feel what they feel. Listening carefully and maintaining a gentle tone of voice and non-aggressive body language are key approaches that help build empathy.

Sincerity

Be honest about how you feel, be true to who you are, but do both in a way that seeks to honour the person with whom you disagree. It is far easier to skirt around conflict and pretend all is OK, but this often leads to gossip and allows bitterness to fester. Sincerity rejects this kind of pretence.

Patience

Recognise that understanding others and relating to them effectively takes time. Bearing with people who see life through a different lens takes time. Patience is one of the hallmarks of respect.

Equality

Treat the person with whom you may disagree with dignity, showing that they are your equal rather than you being above them. Everyone is entitled to their own opinion. To help this, it can be helpful to visualise a challenging conversation before it takes place, imagining you are sitting beside the other person rather than opposite them. Posture is a key means of exemplifying equality.

Courtesy

Show dignity by listening carefully. People may forget what you said but they are unlikely to forget how you made them feel. Acknowledge that hearing them is as important as being heard yourself. This is particularly true when you don't agree with someone.

Truthfulness

Never manipulate the situation through exaggeration or deception. The temptation to do so may be high and often these things come subconsciously. A great deal of leadership respect can be fostered through a resolute determination to tell the truth in every situation.

The aim of leadership ought to be to display the attributes shared above and in so doing seek to empower and develop the other person. Viewed through this lens, conflict can be turned into a powerful force for good. By showing a deep and consistent respect towards others, we are more likely to be respected ourselves.

Nudges

✎ Try to recall a particularly challenging conversation where you felt deeply valued, despite the disagreement? What did the other person do to help you feel this way? What was the impact on your relationship?

✎ Which element of the R.E.S.P.E.C.T. acronym has the greatest potential to help you deal with conflict? Which poses the greatest danger of being a blind spot for you?

✎ Look out for a day-time chat show or the next televised parliamentary debate. Where do you see the principles of this chapter present or absent? Remember, we can learn from bad examples as much as good ones.

CHAPTER 34

THE DANGEROUS SIDESTEP - AVOIDING THE LION, BUT EATEN BY A TIGER

Most people are naturally conflict averse. After all, isn't it far more enjoyable when we just get along with others? Conflict is exhausting, particularly when it triggers emotional responses linked to past hurts. Conflict can leave us feeling misunderstood and unappreciated. Some people are so conflict averse that they will seek to avoid it no matter what the cost, even withholding information out of the desire to protect the other person's feelings. In the long run, this can actually decrease engagement and escalate potential conflict.

There are many perfectly understandable reasons for wanting to avoid conflict, but they can end up being a dangerous sidestep, creating greater problems further down the line, this would be like desperately running from a lion, only to get eaten by the tiger lurking around the corner.

Of course, there can be wisdom in avoiding conflict. We need to learn to let some things go, show forbearance and tolerance, display grace and appreciate difference. Problems arise, however, when we use these positive virtues as a smoke screen for avoiding difficult conversations, causing us and other people to miss vital opportunities to grow.

In many ways, the root of these issues lies in the way we choose to look at conflict. A popular caricature of confrontation is depicted in an image of a red-faced, finger-pointing, shouty, accusatory little man. Confrontation is not about winning or losing but sadly we often frame it as such. Perhaps this is why most of us shy away from it. When confrontation is framed as an argument that must be won, most of us will naturally shy away, particularly if we are up against someone who can shout louder! If winning the argument becomes more important than building understanding, we can damage relationships.

Instead, if conflict is framed as an opportunity for mutual growth, underpinned by respect (see Chapter 33), confrontation can be like green vegetables – gifts that few people want but we all know are good for us! Calm and respectful confrontation can sometimes be the only way of really coming to understand character traits and behaviours in ourselves that are not healthy.

In *Everybody's Normal Till You Get to Know Them*, Pastor John Ortberg speaks of what he calls *"the last 10%"*.[25] He observes that we often go through all the hard work of setting up a

---

[25] John Ortberg, *Everybody's Normal Till You Get to Know Them* (Michigan: Zondervan, 2003), p.142.

difficult conversation, and then in the moment shrink back from saying the hardest but often the most important thing. Fearing conflict, we withhold *"the last 10%"*, failing to see that this is exactly where real growth lies. This principle is not suggesting we seek to straighten out everything in every person we speak to. Rather, it is about guarding against our tendency to evade or hold back precisely when the truth is most needed and difficult to speak. Embracing *"the last 10%"* is choosing temporary pain in place of permanent superficiality.

Here are some suggestions for how we can create cultures that embrace positive conflict:

- Recognise that conflicting opinions + high stakes + strong emotions = crucial conversations.[26] They are inevitable, so we must be prepared to approach them with respect.

- Learn to reflect before responding. Question your own motives.

- Create environments where it is safe to disagree with one another. Focus on the context as much as the conversation.

- Seek to identify common ground wherever possible.

- Describe how you see the situation before seeking to evaluate it.

- Try to avoid inflating conflict to be bigger than it needs to be.

---

[26] See: Paterson, Grenny, McMillan and Switzler, *Crucial Conversations* (New York: McGraw Hill Education, 2012), p2.

- Identify potential pain points (the issue lying at the heart of the conflict) and intentionally go there, choosing to deal with the all the facts, especially the inconvenient ones. This is so often the key to unlocking meaningful conversation.

- Help people to feel safe to disagree with you.

- Be aware of your own tendencies to either throw punches or pull punches. What are the dangers of each?

- Avoid making casual assumptions and sweeping statements.

- Recognise your own shortcomings.

- Commit to being held accountable to decisions that are made in order to avoid misunderstanding further down the track. Commit to being clear on what has been agreed. Who is responsible for what action? When? What will follow-up look like?

One of the marks of a great leaders is the display of consistency in dealing with conflict in a fair and honesty way, looking each time for the growth opportunity. The qualities outlined in Part 2, especially character, humility and authenticity, are key for developing this kind of consistency. Conflict doesn't have to be our enemy as long as it is handled well. How are you currently doing in these areas? What would help you improve?

Nudges

🖊 Where are you in danger of neglecting the last 10% and opting for superficiality rather than speaking the hard truths?

✎ Who do you know who is effective at handling conflict? What have you learnt from them?

✎ What is it about you that might lead another person to want to sidestep around a difficult conversation? What could you do to address this?

CHAPTER 35

GO TO THE SOURCE -
INTEGRITY THAT SAYS "NO!"
TO GOSSIP

Have you ever come across *Mizaru, Kikazaru and Iwazaru*? These are the names of the *Three Wise Monkeys*, depicted in the Japanese proverb "See no evil, hear no evil, speak no evil". You won't find it hard to find carvings or pictures of this trio of primates in craft markets and souvenir shops all over the world.

Whilst most of us would subscribe to the sentiments expressed in this saying, gossip remains a pervasive issue in many teams. We probably all struggle against a tendency to talk *about* others rather than talk *to* them. Gossip erodes trust, breeds insecurity and undermines authority. Gossip breeds toxicity, exaggeration and malice. Gossip is seductive and deceptive, sucking people in without their initial awareness. The challenge for leaders is knowing how to stamp it out.

You may find it helpful to consider the dynamics of gossip:

> Imagine a scenario when Person A is hurt by Person B.
>
> Person A then has a critical choice: go to Person B and confront the behaviour that has caused hurt or go sideways to Person C and gossip.
>
> When Person A chooses the best option and goes to Person B, the conversation is likely to be painful, but the hurt is contained (remember Chapter 34?). If Person A chooses the easier but wrong option and goes sideways to Person C, Person C then has a choice: participate or block.
>
> Participation fuels drama and gossip and ends up being toxic as the gossip rarely remains contained. Everyone loses out. By contrast, blocking the gossip by verbalising a commitment not to even hear it, displays a clear refusal to engage and hands responsibility back to Person A to do the right thing and speak directly to Person B.

The point of the illustration is that *every* person has a responsibility in refusing to allow gossip take root.

Here are a few more observations to ponder:

The best way to deal with gossip (or indeed any potential conflict) is almost always face-to-face. (There are *very* few instances where this would not be the case.) We would be wise to regularly check our motivations. Calling out the hurt we observe the other person have caused must always be motivated by wanting to serve rather than slay them. This builds a healthy culture and states that gossip has *no seat on this bus*. Challenge must never be motivated by a desire to take revenge for past hurt or to impose suppressive influence over another person.

The actual journey of confrontation is also worth considering, seeking to be intentional and clear in order to avoid any misunderstanding. These four steps may prove to be helpful:

1. Describe clearly what you have observed (e.g., *"I have heard about some hurtful comments you have made about me to others after our meeting yesterday."*)

2. Explain how you feel (e.g., *"I feel pretty undermined as it was a confidential discussion, and I was just trying to be honest with you."*)

3. Tell what the consequences have been (e.g., *"I am now being accused of saying things I never said and it's negatively impacting my relationship with others on the team."*)

4. Ask for the change you'd like to see (e.g., *"Please don't do that again as I want to be able to trust you."*)

Notice that these are very clear and deliberate statements, that leave no room for ambiguity. They address the issue head on but in a way that is measured and avoids inflammatory emotion. Notice also the natural flow the statements take.

Leadership integrity that says *"No!"* to gossip has the power to be an incredibly effective tool used to build healthy cultures. Remember this starts with you. Make sure you go to the source next time you have been wronged. Remember to never leave the gossip door ajar.

Nudges

- Where have you experienced someone gossiping about you, grumbling to another person? What was the impact on you? them? the team?

- Think of a time where you have let someone down and they have shown the integrity to come and challenge you directly. How did you respond?

- What might you need to remember next time you are placed in a situation where someone comes to you to complain about another person? What choices do you have in that moment?

CHAPTER 36

EXPOSED YET UNASHAMED - LEARNING TO BUILD TRUST

The focus of the previous three chapters are all crucial for learning to handle conflict well. Building them into the DNA of our leadership will be transformative in relationships. Ultimately what each of these principles helps to build is trust: that firm belief in the reliability, truthfulness, or ability of someone or something.

Trust is an intriguing concept for it takes time to build and yet can be destroyed in only a moment. The famous footballing star Christiano Ronaldo was once interview by Piers Morgan on his *Life Stories* chat show. What was most fascinating to learn was that he only trusted three people completely: his brother, his agent and his wife. This was due to multiple experiences of having confidences broken.

How many people do you trust? Not in a general sense of *'you seem pretty trustworthy'* which is hopefully true of most people but in terms of truly trusting? I suspect you are not too different from Ronaldo. True trust is very precious because it is so rare.

What might it look like for you to foster greater trust amongst those you lead? What might it take for you to trust other people more? What might it take for others to trust you more? Trust has to be built and like anything that is built well, it takes time.

Trust is vital as a foundation for handling conflict because trust helps people feel safe. Safe people have fewer defences and the fewer defences we have, the more honest we feel we can be. Our aim is to get to a place where we are metaphorically exposed yet unashamed, where people can see us with our foibles and rough edges, and we don't feel the need to cover them up or explain them away.

Trust is also essential in the context of mistakes. If trust has been built, our mistakes may still have an impact, but others will be more willing to forgive and move forward. In fact, mistakes can build trust if they are owned instead of being excused or blamed on others.

There are a number of different ways to build trust:

- Ensure conflict is never personal but is instead motivated by a shared resolve to fight for the best outcome and for growth in one another.

- Choose honesty and refuse to sweep your mistakes under the carpet.

- Refuse to be someone who says "*yes*" to a person's face, only then to say "*no*" behind their back moments later. (This is a form of passive aggression[27] and can be hugely damaging).

---

[27] Passive aggression is a means of exhibiting resistance to an idea or agreed commitment in an indirect way. It can be characterised by stubbornness, cynicism, sarcasm or by seeking to manipulate a situation through covertly taking a different course of action to the agreed one.

- Commit to be vulnerable and authentic. It takes courage to fight for a better way. (See Chapter 21).

- Treasure it. Trust is like a precious artefact to be protected and valued.

- Consider the cost to yourself and other people of hiding what is true about yourself. Try to understand why you are hiding the real you from others. What are you trying to protect?

Take a moment to consider past situations of conflict in which you have been involved. What role did trust or a lack of trust play in how conflict was handled? Is there anything you could have done *beforehand* that would have helped lay a stronger foundation of trust? Is there anything you could have done *in the moment* to foster trust? Is there anything you could have done *after* the event to strengthen trust for the future?

Asking these searching questions can be a powerful way of not only recognising the concepts laid out in this chapter, but also ensuring they are put into practice.

Nudges

🖋 In your experience, what behaviours most quickly undermine trust?

🖋 *"You don't always have to like a person or agree with them to be able to trust them."* – Do you agree or disagree? Why?

🖋 This chapter has outlined the relationship between trust and vulnerability. What holds you back from being more vulnerable? How well do you handle other people's vulnerability?

CHAPTER 37

THE POWER OF A PAUSE - WEIGHING CRITICISM BEFORE RESPONDING

Every leader will have to face up to the reality of being criticised. The key is how you handle it. How we respond to challenge and criticism speaks volumes about the kind of leader we are.

No-one likes to be criticised as it can easily trigger emotional responses that make the situation worse. For this reason the best thing a leader can do when they hear criticism is to listen very carefully to what is being said and consider it carefully. There is almost always at least a grain of truth in even the most scathing criticism and we will grow as leaders if we learn to search for it. There is great power in a pause that enables us to weigh criticism before responding. Below are some suggestions of how best to use this pause: four behaviours to avoid and three questions to ask. Which ones speak most clearly to you?

Avoid immediate responses.

Remember the power of a pause. If nothing else, a pause allows your mind to catch up with your emotions and ensures that what comes from you next is helpful.

Avoid inflammatory language.

There are certain words that are worth avoiding, like "*always*" and "*never.*" Without meaning to, we can end up exaggerating or overstating a point, robbing it of both integrity and impact.

Avoid generalisation.

Try to avoid vague comments or phrases that cannot be backed up. A common example of this is: "*Everyone thinks this is a bad idea.*" When questioned about "*everyone*" we get embarrassed because, in reality, we can name only one person! Using generalisation can demotivate people and escalate issues.

Avoid deflection.

Deflection tries to explain away a criticism or, worse still, turn it around as a means of getting back at the person criticising you. Deflection can be a subtle form of pride and undermines integrity. If you challenge me, my responsibility is to handle it appropriately, not to throw it back on you.

Ask yourself why the person may be challenging you.

Understanding their motive and their experience of what has gone before can be a helpful way to diagnose the real issue that may lie deeper than the criticism itself. As an example, how much of the criticism we hear is actually a symptom of a deeper

issue of exhaustion and frustration? If we attend only to the surface issue, the deeper issue is unlikely to get resolved.

Ask yourself what truth is there in the challenge.

Always try to look for the learning. Other people can be a
gift to us, helping us to see ourselves more clearly than we
could on our own. If you are unsure about the validity of
the challenge, ask first for concrete examples that justify the
challenge.

Ask yourself what your motive is before responding.

Ultimately we should be looking to serve the person who has
criticised us. This might be in the humility displayed through
accepting the criticism and resolving to change. Occasion-
ally, we might also be able to help the critic to be a little more
measured in their challenges by accepting the truth in what
they say and also gently exposing any falsehood.

Did you notice that these 'asks' are questions to ask ourselves? There is great power in a pause. The best leaders
remember this.

Nudges

✎ This chapter provided four suggested things to *avoid*
   when challenged by another person and three suggested questions to *ask* in response. Pick one 'avoid'
   and one 'ask' that most stands out to you. Try to recall
   a recent challenging conversation. How might it have
   gone differently if you had avoided the 'avoid' and
   asked the 'ask'?

When you are challenged in a direct and unfair way, what unhelpful response might you need to watch out for in yourself?

Who do you know who has modelled effective ways of responding to criticism? What have you learnt from them?

CHAPTER 38

LOOK FOR THE GROWTH POINT – TURNING EVERY CHALLENGE INTO AN OPPORTUNITY

One of the reasons leadership can be so tiring is because of the constant need to inject energy into what you do. This is necessary to keep yourself motivated but also rubs off on those you lead. Some of the most impactful leaders are those who display an infectiously positive attitude. This attitude is rooted in an inner determination to grow through challenge and is fuelled by perspective.

Perspective involves stepping back from a problem and, in so doing, altering the vantage point from which we view it. Look for a moment at the image below. Is the box spotty or clear? How you answer that question is purely a matter of perspective. It depends on which side of the box you are.

Perspective becomes a key player in our overall leadership mindset. Consider for a moment the difference between the Optimist, the Pessimist and the Realist. Which one best describes you?

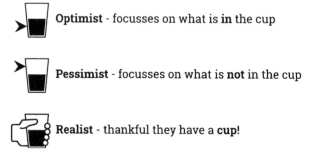

Optimist - focusses on what is **in** the cup

Pessimist - focusses on what is **not** in the cup

Realist - thankful they have a **cup!**

Imagine for a moment that the problem you face as a leader is like a huge mountain looming before you. The optimist launches off to scale the mountain and the realist decides there must be a better way, so sets off to walk around it. The key in both responses is the positive mindset displaying a determination to overcome the obstacle. When you get to the top of a mountain or find another way to get around it, how does it make you feel? What motivational impact does it have on the people around you?

In contrast, the pessimist sits down defeated before they even take their first step and the mountain wins when it need not. A dose of perspective could have become the vital weapon to prevent the pessimist from becoming despondent. Incidentally, perspective could also help the optimist by preventing them charging ahead and wasting needless energy. Perspective could also help the realist recognise that there are multiple alternative routes. Perspective will not objectively change the problem, but it will subjectively change how we view it.

The blessing of perspective opens our eyes to see possible *growth points*: those specific moments we reach in our leadership challenges that present us with opportunity for personal growth. Whilst hardships are by definition not easy, it is through challenges that our character, resolve and skill sets can best develop.

Looking for the growth point in every challenge is hardwired into the DNA of quality leaders. Even operational disasters or significant failures can be used positively for individual and group growth. The key lies in mindset. Optimism, realism and pessimism are all mindset choices. The latter is an attitude of defeat. The former two both provide opportunities for growth.

Spend some time reflecting on each of the scenarios below. What might a possible growth point be in each?

Scenario 1 – You are in a season of life that has become very lonely. No-one around you seems to 'get' the pressures you are under and those who have tried to offer advice haven't really helped.

Scenario 2 – You come out of a meeting in which an unexpected issue was raised, causing conflict between two of the members. The meeting had to end early with the potential for a team split.

Scenario 3 – Having been asked to speak at a key conference, you prepare diligently. On the day, your laptop crashes, you are unable to show your slides and your train of thought becomes interrupted. The whole thing was a bit of a disaster and your reputation and the reputation of the organisation that you represent have been tainted.

Scenario 4 – Work pressures have been building steadily, your friend is dying of cancer and you have not managed to exercise in weeks. You desperately need a break, but there is no obvious end in sight. People you care about would be let down if you stopped spinning all these plates.

The world needs leaders to display an inner determination to make every interaction in life (whether easy or difficult, enjoyable or painful) an experience that will lead to their growth and the growth of those around them. Could this be said of your leadership?

Nudges

✎ Try to recall a recent situation of conflict where opportunities to turn the challenges into moments of growth were missed. What was the impact?

✎ How has your leadership been strengthened through challenge or conflict? Where have you seen this in others?

✎ When the growth is not immediately obvious, how might the principles of mindset and perspective help you?

CHAPTER 39

NEVER JUDGE A BOOK BY ITS COVER – SEARCHING FOR WHAT OTHERS CAN TEACH YOU

Each time a new person walks into a room, we subconsciously make a number of value judgements based on sensory cues including dress sense and posture, first words spoken, tone of voice, gesture and eye contact. On the basis of these split-second judgements, we then decide whether to engage further with the person. It is easy to disengage in a crowded room, but far harder when it is just you and that person.

These judgments create a challenge to us as leaders: to never become indifferent to other people, assuming there is nothing we can learn from them.

We can do little to prevent our initial reaction toward another person. Subconscious reactions are just that: subconscious. The significant moment, however, is the *next* moment. How do we consciously *respond* to the initial subconscious reaction?

Our instincts will normally cause us to gravitate towards people who are more like us. Perhaps this is because these engagements normally require less energy from us. Yet if we never choose to respond differently to our instincts, we will miss significant opportunities to learn from other people, particularly those who are different to us.

Here's a challenge for you: identify a 'nobody' – that is, someone you would not naturally choose to interact with – then be intentional in spending some time with them. What you are likely to discover is that they are indeed *not* a nobody but a somebody; somebody who can teach you something.

Here are three examples:

You choose to step towards Danny. He's socially awkward. He cannot sustain eye contact and is easily distracted. This makes it a tricky conversation, but as you persevere it becomes clear that he is very knowledgeable in a field you are keen to grow in. As the relationship develops, Danny provides you with insights you may never have gleaned if you'd not taken that first step.

You choose to step towards Davina. She is rather angular and brusque, speaking from her heart with few filters. She can come across as rude and arrogant. The most annoying thing for you is her inability to listen. Whilst Davina's behaviours never change, you learn a lot about her manner. This helps you become more self-aware of how you can exhibit similar behaviours. In this way, Davina has helped you to grow.

You choose to step towards Dolly. She doesn't dress like you, talk like you, think like you or relate like you. She is a real eccentric, whilst your life is much more ordered and precise. Her flamboyance feels overwhelming, but you gradually begin to see how perceptive she is. She has some amazingly accurate insights into your own behaviours. She helps you understand your stress triggers. Who'd have thought that she could help you in this way? Stepping towards her has taught you a valuable lesson.

If you want to thrive as a leader, always give people a chance. You will be surprised at what you can learn.

Nudges

✎ Even though it is challenging to walk towards a potentially difficult person, how might it help you to grow as a leader?

✎ What characteristic about you might make it difficult for another person to draw close to you?

✎ Can you think of an example when you have wrongly *'judged a book by its cover'* and later been surprised by the depth of engagement that was possible? How might that experience help you change your mind-set in the future?

CHAPTER 40

SAYING SORRY - THE DISARMING POWER OF AN APOLOGY

Saying *"I'm sorry"* is one of the hardest things any leader will have to do. Doing this *well* is harder still. Benjamin Franklin, one of the Founding Fathers of the United States, once observed *"How few there are who have courage enough to own their faults."* Are you a leader who is one of them?

All leaders will make mistakes. A sincere apology typically has three characteristics. It is humble, honest and heartfelt. This sort of apology involves the right heart posture and is driven by the right attitude as much as anything else. Let's look at each in turn.

A truly humble apology is an incredibly powerful thing to witness.

When did you last make a mistake? Seeing mistakes in others is normally far easier than admitting our own. Growing in self-awareness will help us spot our mistakes and, more importantly, to own them with humility. The opposite involves our pride that either seeks to deny and cover up our mistakes or blames another person for them. A humble apology sees no need for comparison or self-justification. Accepting the mistake for what it is and displaying a desire to absorb the consequences is a key sign. A humble apology refuses to follow with a *"but"*. Even in situations where there are justifying issues, a humble apology doesn't assume the right to trade on this. Humility fosters further humility in the same way that pride fosters further pride. The attractiveness of humility means it is something that can make a lasting impression, long after the actual apology is offered.

The second characteristic of a sincere apology is honesty.

In a world where dishonesty is so pervasive, there is something deeply attractive and disarming about an honest apology. Honesty can diffuse situations of conflict and prevent issues escalating through exaggeration or cover up. Honesty also sets a precedent for future conversations through the way it engenders trust and builds relational capital. Dishonesty may feel like a short-term means to a gain, but it costs you and others far more in the long-term. How different the world would be if we were leaders committed to absolute honesty in all things.

The third characteristic of a sincere apology is that it is heartfelt.

A begrudging, muttered, half-hearted *"sorry"* holds very little transformational power. A heartfelt apology is quite the opposite. The key is avoiding non-threatening or defensive body language and committing to maintaining good eye contact and being deeply relational: *"I'm sorry I made you feel 'X' when I did 'Y'. I can see that I caused you to feel Z. I'm sorry. Will you forgive me?"*

As you continue to reflect on the challenges of this chapter, it may be worth re-reading Chapters 9 and 10 again: *Inner foundations - this thing called character*; and *Sweep the sheds - Humility and the burying of ego*. Character and humility underpin the ability to say sorry in a way that genuinely changes you and most greatly impacts others.

> **Nudges**
>
> 🖊 When did you last admit you were wrong?
>
> 🖊 What do you think is the greatest cost to you when you offer someone a sincere apology?
>
> 🖊 What do you think is the greatest benefit to the person you apologise to?

PART 6

HELPING OTHERS TO LEAD

"People who are truly strong lift others up. People who are truly powerful bring others together."

Michelle Obama Former First Lady

"Leadership is not about title, positions or flowcharts. It is about one life influencing another."

John C. Maxwell American Author and Speaker

"Serve to lead."

Leadership Motto Royal Military Academy Sandhurst

Relationships lie at the heart of leadership. The ability to influence others positively is like throwing a rock into a lake – the ripples keep on going. Being a catalyst for the growth of others is a crucial ingredient for effective leadership and is a hallmark of a great leader. Building teams and developing other people can be a daunting task and requires great patience. People change slowly. Growing leaders requires commitment for the long haul. Perhaps that is why this development is rare. The key question every leader ought to ask is this: *"Who am I taking the responsibility to develop?"* The final part of this book will help us think about this.

CHAPTER 41

UNDER THE MICROSCOPE - LEADING OTHERS WELL BY LEADING YOURSELF FIRST

Leading others well so that they can grow is a crucial responsibility and a privilege for any leader. To do this, we must first lead ourselves well. A great deal of leadership influence comes via example. This means that consistently demonstrating positive leadership is as important as talking about it. Remember, reputation takes a long time to build and can be destroyed in a moment.

Leadership comes with responsibility. Leaders are rightly under more scrutiny, constantly under the microscope. It is vital that we are clear about who we are and how we want to behave. Reminding yourself of the issues discussed in Parts 1 and 2 may be helpful at this point.

Below are five areas to consider that will help you lead yourself well in order to lead others:

Growth

Talk to any gardener and they will tell you that healthy things grow. No matter how experienced we may be, we all have room for growth. The question is, "What are we doing to become healthier and keep growing?" Just as a plant needs H_2O and CO_2 and light for growth, there are vital inputs that we need in order to grow as leaders. Who do you spend time with? What do you read or listen to? How do you relax? Do you eat well and get enough exercise? Are you a leader committed to your own growth? Being intentional in these things is like carefully considering where and when you plant a seed, making all the difference to the plant's ongoing health and growth.

Influence

You do not have to be *the* leader to lead. Any person can have a positive influence in any moment. By committing to regularly leading ourself well, we will ensuring we remain in the best possible place from which to exert positive influence when opportunities arise.

Flexibility

Leadership requires agility and the ability to adapt to ever-changing circumstances. It is not about having pre-determined response plans but more the right mindset and behaviours to respond optimally. When faced with a personal challenge, the effective leader doesn't simply declare, "*This is not working.*" Instead she says, "*This is not working the way we are doing it.*" The difference is significant. Our growth as a leader is unlikely ever to be linear. Therefore, we may need to adjust our attitude or the influences over us in order to maximise our growth in any given moment. If we are not growing in the ways that we had hoped, what small changes could we make to help better facilitate the changes we want to see in ourselves?

Resilience

Sir Winston Churchill is famed for declaring the need to *"never ever give up!"* Perseverance will be necessary as most people grow slowly and this can be frustrating. Persevering with your own growth will enable you to persevere with helping other people grow.

Patience

Most people change slowly, but it is the steady slow growth that produces the greatest depth. Fast growth can look impressive on the outside but can lack substance. As the old adage goes: *"How do you eat an elephant? Answer: One bite at a time."* Never forget that small incremental change is still change. Patience provides perspective and good leadership regularly requires this. Imagine that leading yourself poorly is positioned on the far left and leading yourself well is on the far right. Why not challenge yourself each day simply to take one more step to the right?

A team will only be as healthy as the leader wants it to be. In the same way, leaders themselves will only be as healthy as they determine to be. What does this look like for you?

Nudges

✎ In what area of your life do you feel you best lead yourself? Why?

✎ In what area of your life do you feel you lead yourself less well? Why?

✎ Try to name one concrete action that will help you today to take one step to the right in leading yourself better.

CHAPTER 42

STRONGER TOGETHER - BUILDING HEALTHY TEAMS

We have all heard the phrase *"there is no 'I' in TEAM."* We may also have been in teams where one ego that pipes up *"but there is in WINNER."* I hope that ego is never you! True leadership has at its core a 'we' not 'me' mentality. The dangers for many leaders are that we spend too much time doing and not enough time leading.

Effective leadership requires the ability to build healthy teams, convinced that we can be stronger together. Team building requires every member of the team to be able to say with conviction *"I need you and you need me."* This involves a tacit commitment to creating a chorus and not a solo. Whilst teams may not move as quickly as individuals (at least until momentum is built), effective teams will go further than individuals. As leaders we don't need to know everything and we can't do everything. We don't have inexhaustible energy. None of us is self-sustaining nor self-sufficient. We need each other.

Healthy teams are incredibly energising places to be. I've been in two and I loved it. They were founded on mutual trust, a crystal clear purpose (what I call a team's "*why*") and the recognition that every person mattered and could contribute. The team's purpose was memorable and visible. This made it unavoidable. By way of contrast, unhealthy teams can be demoralising. Such teams are founded on control, a lack of clarity and pride. If indeed the heart of leadership is relationships, how might this play out in the way we both lead and contribute to teams?

A common way to build healthy teams is through specific team-building exercises, psychometric profiling[28] and specific training days. I recommend all of these. However, they must never be a replacement for the day-to-day commitment of *being* a healthy team. Our regular behaviours are the most powerful means of building or undermining heathy teams.

The way we run or contribute to meetings is one of these key behaviours but how much do we think about *how* we run them? What impact do your meetings have on team building? I recently read an article in the *Harvard Business Review* in which the author outlined four purposes of a meeting: 1. Influence people, 2. Make decisions, 3. Solve problems, 4. Strengthen relationships. I suspect our focus is often disproportionally on the first three. The fourth purpose is perhaps

---

[28] There are numerous Psychometric Profiling tools to consider, each with their benefits. I would suggest that the most effective is C-me Colour Profiling: www.colour-profiling.com. C-Me focusses on behaviours instead of personality, the former being what has the greatest impact on others; it utilises a highly accurate algorithm; and it generates reports that are clear and memorable. (More information can be found at the back of this book).

not as tangible or measurable, but where it is recognised it will undoubtedly add value to the other three purposes.

Great teams do not have to be full of best friends; they just have to be full of people who want to help get the best out of each other. One great way to intentionally strengthen relationships in your team is to have what I call an *'appreciation round table'* every six to twelve months. Here's how it works: each team member takes a turn to be the focus, and the other members take it in turns to tell that member something they most appreciate about what they bring to the team. The only rule is that the person receiving these encouragements must listen carefully and then accept the appreciation with a heartfelt *"thank you"* - without additional comment or deflection. It is a powerful way of learning to hear and accept encouragement. Although at first this might feel awkward, when done well it can have a phenomenal impact.

A second suggestion is to build in time which is deliberately 'off task and away' from a work setting, to enable you to have fun together over a shared experience. What might this look like in your context?

If you feel your team's culture is not as strong as it could be, commit to playing your part in bringing about the change you want to see. In one sense, a team's culture is only ever as strong as the team wants it to be. Is your team one where it is safe to speak up and where people own their mistakes? Since culture is caught as much as taught, you can lead a change in culture without being *the* leader. It has to start somewhere. Perhaps it could start with you?

Nudges

✎ What is the primary contribution you make to the team(s) you are in?

✎ What do you lack in character, attitude, behaviour or skills? Are there others around you who might support you in these areas?

✎ Consider the power of being a leader who has the humility to say, "*I need your help.*" Also consider how your leadership is helping to foster environments in which others feel safe to share their struggles.

CHAPTER 43

TALK IS CHEAP – ENSURING VALUES ARE OWNED AND LIVED OUT

Value statements are a means of communicating what is most important to you, your team or your organisation. They drive behaviour and determine what actions are best. Values are a means of distilling purpose and joy and hope. The problem with value statements is that they often remain theoretical, sounding impressive on paper, perhaps stuck on a wall looking pretty, but then not lived out. This means they never serve as more than memorable soundbites. Rhetoric must become reality. Our values must be lived out consistently if they are genuinely to shape culture in a positive way. [29] It is also important that your values cost you something; that they are valuable. This will help you treasure them. To help with this, here are two suggestions to reflect on.

---

[29] To reflect on this more deeply, I would thoroughly recommend the following article: Patrick Lencioni. "Make Your Values Mean Something". *Harvard Business Review*, July 2002. Available at: www.hbr.org/2002/07/make-your-values-mean-something. Accessed 22 February 2021.

Firstly, it is a healthy practise to ensure that everyone in your team or organisation can *name* your shared values without hesitation. You'd be amazed at the number of people who cannot name these values on the spot. Secondly, as important as articulating your values is also considering *specific behaviours* that support these values. How could you then weave them into everything you do? To help you make this a concrete exercise, here is a possible structure to follow, with examples given in *italics*:

Team Value: *Integrity*

Three behaviours that support this value:

1. *We commit to always telling the truth*
2. *We will own our mistakes*
3. *If we don't agree, we promise to speak up*

A behaviour to avoid that would undermine this value: Covering up mistakes, hoping they will be overlooked.

If you feel this structure could help you, why not give it a go? Try not to have too many values as a team. Whilst there may be many things you value, it is best to seek to distil them down to three to five *key* values that are memorable. (Looking at what collectively angers or frustrates you can sometimes provide clues as to what you value most as a team. So too can identifying what you regularly celebrate as a team).

As is often said, *talk is cheap*. Bad habits can multiply just as fast, if not faster, than good ones. Values must therefore be owned if they are to be lived out consistently. Values must be both visible to external observers and felt by the team or a disconnect will occur. One of the most common places for this to happen is in meetings, which are the perfect environment for our values to be either lived out positively or exposed as empty.

Below are six observable behaviours for effective and ineffective meetings. They illustrate many of the values shared in this book so far. How do the meetings you lead or participate in compare?

Effective Meetings

- There is a commitment to preparing well *before* the meeting and coming to the table ready to participate.

- The right people are in the room. The key question for each participant is this: *"What unique contribution can I bring to this moment?"* Meetings ought not to have passive passengers.

- The right questions are asked with the right people answering them.

- Each person is actively involved. (This doesn't mean each person needs to be encouraged to speak on every point. The discipline of *not* speaking is often the biggest contribution certain characters can make to a meeting.)

- Each person commits to *listening* to one another. (Remember the principles laid out in Chapters 18 and 26.) Personal agendas can be laid aside and an outcome found that best serves the team.

- There are clear actions to follow-up that are personally owned with accountability to agreed deadlines.

Ineffective Meetings

- There is no clarity or shared understanding of the purpose of the meeting. What a specific meeting is for is as much about what it is not for. It's foolish to try to achieve too much in an individual meeting. Without clear purpose it is easy to lose the big picture and get bogged down in unnecessary detail.

- Valuable time is used up sharing information. Most of this can be done *before* a meeting. The focus of meetings is to share opinion and make decisions rather than to exchange information. This is a particularly important principle to help get the most out of reflective characters. Some people simply do not respond well when required to share personal opinions without having sufficient time to reflect and prepare first.

- The Chairperson wrongly insists on leading every item.

- Too much time is spent talking and not enough spent listening. Try to avoid the temptation to fill silences. Reflective characters need time to filter information and process their thoughts.

- So much focus is on the agenda and 'getting business done' that personal relationships are overlooked. How we treat one another in meetings is crucial to living out our values.

- There is a lack of clear outcomes and actions. This leads to unnecessary follow-up meetings with little actual progression. Watch out for the *"We'll come back to that next time"* phrase. At times it will be wise to park issues and come back to them after greater reflection, but this phrase is often used as a smokescreen for not being prepared to make tough decisions.

Leaders have a vital role to play in setting the tone through owning and living out team values. How are you getting on?

Nudges

✎ Where have you witnessed '*cheap talk*' that has failed to materialise into action? What do you think could be the primary cause of this?

✎ What steps could you take when you next gather with your team to ensure that strengthening relationships is as great a priority as completion of the meeting agenda?

✎ Where have you experienced good leadership in terms of the preparation *before* a meeting and the follow-up *after* it?

CHAPTER 44

THE WAY WE DO THINGS AROUND HERE - BUILDING HEALTHY CULTURE

As we saw in the previous chapter, values underpin the culture of a team or organisation. Culture is often described as *"the way we do things around here"* and is shaped by shared values that are consistently lived out. You will be able to recall experiences of being in various teams and the sense of whether the culture was healthy or unhealthy. Healthy cultures are vital for growth. Unhealthy cultures breed stagnation at best and decline at worst.

One way to understand the relative health or ill-health of a team's culture is to ask someone outside the team to describe what he or she sees and feels when invited in. We all have blind spots and once 'inside', they can be hard to spot. Make it your regular habit to review your culture and don't be scared of asking for brutal honesty. Make the most of times when new people join your team. Their fresh perspectives can be invaluable.

A second way to reflect on your team's culture is to think carefully about the language that is used to define and affirm the kind of culture you are aiming to build. Language is a powerful means of carrying a culture. The words and phrases we use quickly rub off on others, as long as they are used appropriately and consistently. We overlook the subtle power of language at our peril. It is also true that organisational culture can be sensed without always being spoken about. Vibrant cultures have an air of being *'up to something'* and this makes them inspiring to be a part of.

Here are a few questions to help you consider how you use language.

1. What words or phrases does your team or organisation commonly use that positively motivate people?

2. What language could be used that is more memorable; more *sticky* if you like?

3. How can you avoid using unnecessary clichés?

4. Does the language you use work internally only or could it be used with equal impact when talking to those on the outside?

5. When was the last time you invited a new team member to contribute to the way your culture is described?

A third way to reflect on the culture of the team(s) you lead is to consider the 3 C's: Clarity, Consistency and Courage.

Clarity - Be clear on the expectations that surround the kind of culture you are seeking to nurture.

Consistency - Living out the values that underpin the culture is vital. Without consistency, values get watered down or lost and cultures get eroded. Consider feeding forward as much as feeding back. Feed-back focusses on the past. Whilst it has a vital role to play in reviewing what has been, feedback tends to be reactive. By contrast, feeding forward focusses on future potential and is therefore more proactive. When inconsistency is identified, it may be important to look back at how the circumstances played out (feed-back), and then look ahead to the next opportunity with a firm commitment to approach it differently (feed-forward).

Courage - Clarity and consistency are upheld by courage which calls them out when they are absent. Courage must be a collective commitment. A team is as weak as its weakest member and, if one member is not committed to being courageous, this will be the link that opens the door for cultural slip.

A fourth way to reflect on team culture is to consider dysfunctions that can undermine healthy teams. Patrick Lencioni, in his book *5 Dysfunctions of a Team,*[30] speaks of the dynamics that can undermine healthy teams. The first two of his 'dysfunctions' - *Absence of Trust* and *Fear of Conflict* (see the table below) - are particularly critical in relation to culture. To avoid these dysfunctions, your team needs values that uphold the opposite. Absence of trust can be overcome by valuing honesty. Fear of conflict can be overcome by valuing integrity. The challenge when seeking to build healthy cultures is to ensure there is a commitment to certain behaviours that uphold the values (see Chapter 43). Without the associated *behaviours*, values remain static.

---

[30] Patrick Lencioni, *The Five Dysfunctions of a Team: a leadership fable* (San Francisco: Jossey-Bass, 2002), pp.187-190.

The table below puts this together. For each of the five dysfunctions, a value is given that combats it, along with a behaviour to uphold the value.

DYSFUNCTION	VALUE Combats dysfunction	BEHAVIOUR Upholds value
Absence of Trust	Honesty	Commit to telling the truth and owning mistakes without fear.
Fear of Conflict	Integrity	Commit to keeping short accounts and dealing with relational niggles quickly.
Lack of Commitment	Vision	Reinforce the vision regularly in order to maintain team alignment.
Avoidance of Accountability	Feedback	Ensure regular honest feedback is given clearly and received humbly.
Inattention to Results	Focus	Avoid all unnecessary distractions and learn to say "no."

Which of these dysfunctions are you currently dealing with as a team? What alternatives could help overcome these issues? Most importantly, what behaviours do you need to commit to *together* in order to live out your values consistently?

Nudges

🖊 In Chapter 36 we looked at trust in relation to handling conflict. Trust is also vital for building healthy cultures. Where have you witnessed this? What impact does it have on the team?

🖊 In what ways could you modify some of your own behaviours in order to help those around you to trust you more deeply?

🖊 Cultures are built when there is clarity, consistency and courage. Which of these is strongest in the team / organisation you are a part of? Which has the most room for growth?

CHAPTER 45

DEALERS IN HOPE – THE POWER OF ENCOURAGEMENT

Encouragement is that funny little thing that is easily over-looked despite being extremely powerful. A huge impact can be made with only a little bit of encouragement. Whether it be a handwritten note, a text, an arm round the shoulder or a public acknowledgment of thanks, encouragement is like a gift that keeps on giving. Often it can be the little thing that re-inspires someone who is discouraged or affirms someone who is feeling unnoticed. I can remember words of encouragement shared with me 10, 20, even 30 years ago – they have stuck.

The nineteenth century French statesman and military leader, Napoleon Bonaparte, spoke of leaders being *"dealers in hope."* Encouragement is placing courage within a person (en-courage-ment), thus providing hope.

As you consider what encouragement could look like in your leadership, it may be helpful to think of it in terms of attitude, vision and wisdom.

Attitude

Sir Winston Churchill spoke of attitude as being *"the little thing that makes a big difference."* The attitude of a leader is vital as it sets the tone for all those who follow. Attitudes shape perspective and process. A positive attitude can re-frame a problem and present it as an opportunity. A positive attitude can also have a profound impact on those around us.

In many ways our attitude is a choice. Viktor Frankl in his bestselling book, *Man's Search for Meaning,* believed that *"the last of the human freedoms is to choose one's attitude to any given set of circumstances."*[31] He is more qualified than most to speak about this, being one of the rare survivors of the holocaust. Forced to spend years in solitary confinement, it was his attitude that underpinned the resilience and fortitude he needed to lead himself well during those horrific periods of suffering. Whilst there is a need for realism in leadership, there are plenty of occasions when leaders are required to display what some people call *unwarranted optimism*. Although circumstances may be dire, true leadership has that ability to inspire confidence in the midst of trouble.

If others were asked to describe your attitude in one word, what would they say?

Vision

Bill Hybels describes vision as *"painting a picture of the future that produces passion."*[32] A compelling vision is something that pulls you and others in a particular direction. There is no

---

[31] Viktor Frankl, *Man's Search for Meaning* (London: Ebury Publishing, 2004), p.9.

[32] Bill Hybels, *Courageous Leadership* (Michigan: Zondervan, 2009), p.32.

need to be pushed. When day-to-day activities are connected to a wider vision, the pull action occurs naturally. This operates even more strongly when vision is co-created rather than imposed from above.

Vision involves beginning with the end in mind. Imagine for a moment you wanted to build a racing super-yacht to win a round-the-world maritime race. You obviously require an amazing boat, but you also require a crew with amazing attitudes. Gathering the raw materials and drawing up plans would not be your first task. First you would inspire the team by showing them the vastness of the ocean and encouraging them to imagine the feeling of winning. This is vision.[33]

Vision is about keeping perspective by focussing on the bigger picture. Where are we *right now*? Where are we trying to get *to*? The team can then define the journey, coming up with specific concrete targets (rather than loose abstract concepts). Vison is crucial in driving towards a target. You can often spot a visionary leader by the way they are always

---

[33] Effective leaders have the ability to see around corners: shaping the future and not just reacting to it. They think in terms of *'here to there.'* Henry Ford, the great American entrepreneur, is a great example of this. If he had asked people what they wanted, they might have said "*a faster horse!*" Ford's genius was thinking beyond this and designing the world's first mass car-production plant in 1913.

William Wilberforce was another wonderfully visionary leader. In 1789 he stood before the British Parliament calling for an abolishment to the slave trade. He painted a picture of a different future. A better future. Each year for the next eighteen years his bill was rejected by MPs. His attitude and vision drove him on as he continued his tireless campaign. Amazingly in 1833 Parliament passed a bill that abolished slavery. This was just four days before Wilberforce's death. He held to his vision to the day he died.

asking *"why"* and not becoming unnecessarily distracted by the *"what."*

There is a paradox, however, to vision. Though it is focussed on the bigger picture, it can only move forward one step at a time. The former coach for the Ireland Rugby Team was the New Zealander, Joe Schmidt, who was known to say *"win the moment in front of your face."* Clear vision sets the target and drives you forward to taking the next step, however small.

If any member of your team was asked to articulate the team's vision, could they do this clearly and concisely?

Wisdom

Encouragement requires passion but also wisdom. Wisdom grounds vision and ensures an appropriate pace for change. Wisdom enables the leader to think about communication tactics and to encourage it in a way that will not only inspire the long-term vision but also present attainable steps toward that goal. In Chapter 28 we were reminded that resistance to change is often caused by a lack of clarity, as much as disagreement. Wisdom guides effective leaders as they build bridges which become vital mechanisms for persuasion and encouragement.

There is also an appropriate timeliness that comes with wisdom. As the Biblical proverb declares, *"Timely advice is lovely, like golden apples in a silver basket."*[34] How might you be able to sharpen the way you encourage others so that it is wise as well as passionate?

---

[34] *The Bible,* Proverbs 25:11, New Living Translation, Tyndale House Foundation, 2015.

Nudges

✐ Hope-filled leaders require attitude, vision and wisdom. Who do you know who epitomises these things?

✐ What vision for a better future burns most strongly in your heart? How might some of the ideas in this chapter help you share this vision more clearly with others?

✐ Do you know any discouraged leaders? What practical steps could you take today to be a 'dealer in hope' for them?

CHAPTER 46

GET OUT OF YOUR BOX – LEARNING NEVER STOPS

A quality leader has a growth mindset:[35] a hunger to keep on learning irrespective of how experienced or senior you may become. A growth mindset includes the desire to expand your horizons daily by exposure to different environments, as well as the kind of curiosity that opens locked doors and is prepared to walk into a room where no one is like you. You can spot such a person a mile off. They are uncomfortable with being comfortable. Are you a leader who wants to regularly disrupt yourself? This discomfort will be the catalyst for so much growth.

The most experienced leaders are not always the most effective leaders. Experience only becomes effective if it is guided by three controls. Experience must be anchored in humility, must fuel ongoing learning, and must seek to apply that learning. Without these three controls, experience can lead

---

[35] This phrase was popularised in Carol Dweck's book, *Mindset: The New Psychology of Success* (New York: Ballantine Books), 2007.

to ineffectiveness through the formation and engraining of bad habits.

Dan Pink in his book *Drive* speaks of the danger of what he calls *"functional fixedness"* – the struggle to solve problems due to a fixed mentality of how things have always been done. He also touches on this issue in his July 2009 TED Talk, *The Puzzle of Motivation.*[36] In the talk he describes the *"candle experiment"* conducted by Karl Dunker in 1945. Participants were given a candle, a box of drawing pins and a match. Their task was to attach the candle to the wall so that it would not drip wax on the table. Some tried to pin the candle to the wall. Others tried to melt one end of the candle and stick it to the wall. Both approaches failed. Then someone decided to use a few pins to secure the pin box to the wall and use this as a candle holder. Thus, the task was successfully completed. In this example, functional fixedness was the inability of most people to see the box as anything more than a means of containing the pins.

In order to develop 'outside the box thinking' we need regularly to get out of our boxes. It takes great self-awareness to avoid the tendency to think of leadership only through our own lens. What might it look like for you to get out of the box? You might seek out someone or something that will force you to become uncomfortable. Embracing this relative discomfort is likely to help you grow. Maybe it involves committing to listen to ideas that really make you think – not just opinions that make you feel good or affirm what you already know. You might seek out a nurturing relationship that will enrich your thinking and broaden your perspective.

---

[36] Accessed 23rd February 2021.

Scientists tell us that we have extraordinary levels of untapped *brain plasticity,* an under-developed brain power with much untapped room for growth.[37] As we are exposed to unfamiliar tasks and experiences, our brains develop deeper and more complex roadways and bridges. As the world becomes a web of ever-growing interconnectedness, breadth of perspective and experience will undoubtedly benefit the leader.[38] Remember, this growth is not just for your benefit but has the potential for positively influencing other leaders as well.

Life-long learning enables us to broaden our perspectives, providing us with more flexibility and experience to draw upon when problem-solving. Life-long learning helps keep us mentally supple and fluid in our thinking, encouraging us to maintain a posture of observation and willingness to ask questions or ask for help. This type of learning constantly urges us to find new things (big and small) to challenge us. Learning comes not only from the big moments in life, but also from the accumulation of all the micro-moments. We need to regularly ask ourselves what we need to learn, unlearn and relearn. Learning never stops!

---

[37] Ann Hermann-Nehdi is a helpful thought-leader in the fields of learning and thinking styles and the impact this can have on performance. The focus of her work is on the practical application of neuroscience to enable untapped learning potential to be leveraged. Information on her work can be viewed here: blog.thinkherrmann.com/author/ann-herrmann-nehdi.

[38] David Epstein, *Range: How Generalists Triumph in a Specialised World* (London: Pan Books, 2020). I would thoroughly recommend this very helpful book which speaks to this observation with great perception. I was directed to this book by Bill Gates's blog, www.gatesnotes.com/books which always provides helpful suggestions of worthwhile books to read.

Some learning can come through media of just *'Googling it.'* Yet I'd encourage you to supplement this with a commitment to keep on reading books. This may seem old fashioned to some, but it will help you slow down. It is so easy with media to click away before really engaging with information. Books require more careful thought and a commitment to engage deeply with perspective rather than just picking out sound-bites. I'd encourage you to read books that will stretch you. Find authors with differing perspectives to your own who will offer their insights as well as provide challenge. If we only ever engage with ideas from within our own 'tribes,' we will flatline at best and at worst we will reinforce a narrow-ness that will significantly stunt our leadership.

Nudges

- Are there areas of your own leadership that could be suffering from what Dan Pink calls "functional fixed-ness"? What steps could you take to overcome this?

- What has been the most stimulating experience in your life so far where you have been exposed to new ideas or ways of doing things?

- If you were to recommend three books to a person keen to continue as a life-long leader, what would they be? (If you don't read much but would like to lead more, who might point you in a helpful direction?)

CHAPTER 47

GET OUT OF THE WAY – IDENTIFYING AND RELEASING POTENTIAL IN OTHERS

Growing up I loved playing in the stream near to where we lived. The most memorable challenge my friend and I set ourselves was to try to build a dam and stop the stream flowing. As water slowly piled up behind our constructed wall of mud and stones, we felt a huge satisfaction in pulling out the 'plug rock' and seeing the powerful mass of water surge forwards. If you apply this illustration to leadership, too many leaders fail to get out of the way and end up being like the 'plug rock' - the blockage that prevents a release of potential in others. Giving space for the growth of other leaders requires a surrender of personal control. Focussing on developing leaders rather than gathering followers can be a helpful means to this end.[39]

---

[39] L. David Marquet, *Turn the Ship Around: A True Story of Turning Followers into Leaders* (New York: Penguin Business, 2012). This book is a helpful example of leaders creating leaders. The questions at the end of the each chapter are probably the most significant contribution to the book.

Effective leaders develop the ability to identify and release potential in others, thus becoming multipliers. They are often recognised by their particular commitment to developing the next generation. Below are six areas that are foundational to leader succession.

First, in order to release potential in others we must not be threatened by it.

There are too many sad stories of proud leaders who end up holding others back through a desire to protect their own egos. If you are an experienced leader, it is always important to watch your attitude in this regard. One way to do this is to consider if you always have to be in the room for every meeting. Physically getting out of the way can be an important step in allowing the leadership of others to blossom. This is particularly true for those leaders with a particularly strong presence and influence.

The converse is also true. If you are a less experienced leader, it is worth considering how you might welcome the input of those with more experience, helping you to avoid coming across as a threat. There is a delicate balance to find as a young leader between leading and learning. If you feel held back, try to channel the frustration into leading yourself as well as you can, looking to make a wise judgement about how long to stay where you are.[40]

---

[40] John Maxwell, *The 21 Irrefutable Laws of Leadership,* Chapter 1 The Law of the Lid (Nashville: Thomas Nelson, 2nd Ed., 2007). This book by John Maxwell provides some helpful thinking on individual leadership capacity. He states that every leader has a limit or ceiling to their leadership ability (what he terms their *Lid*). If this lid is not expanded, a leader is likely to stagnate and become unable to lead another person with a greater leadership ceiling. This explains why some leaders feel frustratingly held back when less able leaders are leading them. It takes a truly humble leader to acknowledge their lid and step aside at the right time.

Second, we need to learn to relinquish personal control and suitably empower others.

A power exists in leadership that can be subtly destructive if we hold on to it too firmly. Learning to let go is a vital skill to master and takes great strength of character. By rejecting the natural impulse to take control, we become better placed to release the potential in others. One of the most effective empowerment tools is to resist the urge to solve other people's problems and instead, cultivate the art of asking brilliant questions. Start by asking what energises them. Then try to use the power of questions to coach them to find answers to their own problems. Over time, their felt need to turn to you for validation will decrease.

Empowerment also involves encouragement. Leaders need to believe in their people more than their people sometimes believe in themselves. This belief creates a positive pull, encouraging people step up. It is amazing how much potential can be unleased simply through the power of believing in someone.

Third, we need to be patient.

Developing others takes time, particularly if we are focussed as much on developing their characters as their abilities. Have you ever noticed that it is much easier to develop strategies than it is to develop people? For this reason, it is vital that we choose to step towards the harder task and stick at it. According to a 2016 Gallup poll, ~~a few~~ a huge proportion of millennials prefer on-the-job training.[41] This suggests

---

[41] Gallup. "How Millennials Want to Work and Live: The Six Big Changes Leaders have to Make", *Gallup*, 2016. Available at: www.gallup.com/workplace/238073/millennials-work-live.aspx. Accessed: 18th February 2021.

the need to be intentional in maximising everyday training opportunities, integrating them into regular work flows, rather than boxing them into one-off workshops. Is the training and empowerment of others central to your leadership or do you view it as an optional extra?

Fourth, we need to make leadership development a non-negotiable priority.

Our busyness can quickly become an excuse, but waiting for a 'quieter period' can end up becoming the illusive shadow we chase forever. Making this a priority is largely a mindset choice. We must build into our schedules the commitment to developing others. A helpful question to ask yourself is whether you are primarily focussed on being a D.O.T. or a D.O.P – a *Doer-Of Tasks* or a *Developer-Of-People*.

It might be helpful to consider the presence or absence in your team of what I call a *'growth track'*. Do you have an intentional system and strategy for spotting leadership gifting and then feeding it? The former is the easy part but without the latter, much human potential will remain underdeveloped at best, and simply wasted at worst.

See also: Amy Adkins and Brandon Rigoni. "Millennials Want Jobs to Be Development Opportunities", *Gallup*, June 30, 2016. Available at: www.gallup.com/workplace/236438/millennials-jobs-development-opportunities.aspx. Accessed: 18th February 2021. The three principle findings of this report are as follows: 1. Development is a top factor in retailing millennials, 2. Millennials value development more than other generations do, 3. A majority of millennials are not getting opportunities to learn.

Fifth, we must be prepared to step aside when the time is right.

Seeking the counsel of those you really trust is really important because most of us need to get out of the way sooner
than we might think. There are three possible 'step aside'
times:

1. Too late = disaster.
2. When your replacement is needed = OK.
3. Before your replacement is needed = optimal.

The reason the third option is optimal in that it gives space
and time for the replacement to grow into a role. Ideally the
seasoned leader would work alongside their successor during this period, finding a healthy balance between support
and challenge.

Sixth, when we step aside, we ought to avoid seeking a clone of ourselves.

The type of leadership that one season requires is rarely the
exact type of leadership needed for the next. Rather than trying to find a replacement in our own image, we would be
wiser to ask what the next season requires.

Seventh, when it comes to supporting our successor, we must not assume we know what they most need from us.

Why not ask them? The difference between being a genuine help and a very real hindrance could simply be down to
whether or not we ask this very simple question: *"What kind
of support from me would you find most effective?"*

The following Support-Challenge Matrix below is a useful visual:

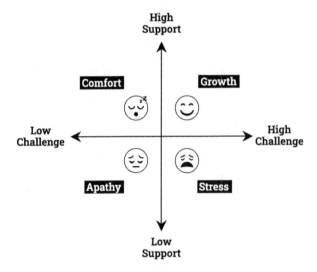

Low Support and Low Challenge leads to apathy.

High Support and Low Challenge leads to comfort.

Low Support and High Challenge leads to stress.

High Support and High Challenge leads to growth.

How could these ideas shape your approach to releasing the potential in others?

Working on these seven foundations will help you grow as a leader focussed on identifying and releasing potential in others.

Nudges

✎ Have you ever felt held back as a leader? What did this feel like?

✎ Is it possible that you could be unintentionally holding anyone back yourself? What are the attitudes that could lie behind this?

✎ Think of someone you could intentionally seek to develop as a leader. Will your mentoring be solely to instruct others or also to learn yourself? What could you intentionally do to reap the potential rewards of the latter?

CHAPTER 48

IT'S NOT ABOUT YOU – GROWING LEADERS WHO SERVE

During the recent hotly contested 2020 presidential election in America, the BBC expressed this of the eventual winner:

> *"The new President-elect has been dreaming of the White House for most of his fifty years in the public arena. With this prize of a lifetime, however, come the challenges of a lifetime."*[42]

Did you notice the immediate problem with this sentiment? As soon as we start viewing leadership as a prize or position, we take our first step away from being effective leaders. Leadership must not be judged solely on the basis of exploits completed, deals done and legacy left. These things might

---

[42] BBC News, *"US Election 2020: Time for US to unite, President-elect Biden says"*, BBC News Online, 7 November 2020. Available at: www.bbc.co.uk/news/election-us-2020-54836636 Accessed February 25, 2021. Accessed: 25th February 2021.

be markers and, in the right context, celebrated. Yet the true assessment of leadership ought to be the extent to which a leader has served others.

Here are some questions to reflect on:

> Who has benefitted from your leadership?
>
> How would they describe the way you have led them?
>
> Where have you released potential in others?
>
> Where have you acknowledged your limits and stepped back to enable others to step up?
>
> How has your attitude been a model to the next generation?
>
> How have you inspired them?

Leadership ought to be viewed as a craft: something to be constantly refining and reflecting on. Although certain people clearly have a discernible leadership gift, every person is called in one way or another to be a leader. As we have seen, this starts with leading ourselves well. Leadership by definition means there are people to be led. This makes it an inherently relational task.

Boiled down to its most simple, leadership is a choice to enter into life-giving relationships with others. Its aim: to influence their characters, attitudes and behaviours in order to see personal and collective transformation. This is a mind-set more than anything else. Mindset is a choice. This does not mean it is easy, but it is still a choice.

Jesus Christ is the most influential and well-known leader who ever lived. His definition of himself as a leader:

"I have not come to be served but to serve."[43]

Imagine a world where every leader is committed to this vision, leading in such a way that it is not about them. Our world needs leaders who are full of the right stuff: servant leaders who enable others to flourish. Are you going to be one of them?

Nudges

🖊 Who is the most servant-hearted leader you have ever witnessed? What strikes you most about their leadership?

🖊 *"Leadership is all about relationships"* – what could this mean for your priorities over the coming month?

🖊 What is the single most helpful thought you have gained from reading this book? Whom could you positively influence by passing your learning on?

---

[43] *The Bible*, Mark 10:45, New International Version, Hodder and Stoughton, 1984.

EPILOGUE

I'm ~~not~~ a leader.

I hope you are convinced and over time will learn to release the leader within you. I hope those around you will be committed to helping you as well. Equally I hope you will be committed to supporting them. Working together in this way will transform leadership in our world, which in turn will transform our world.

A commitment to the sort of leadership described in this book will involve three things.

Firstly, this kind of commitment will be a **choice**.

It will be a choice that every person needs to make, and is first and foremost a commitment to leading ourselves well. This is our greatest challenge. We also have a choice of how we will relate to others. Never forget that leadership is all about positively influencing others through relationships.

Secondly, this kind of commitment will be **costly**.

Servant-hearted leadership is not as widespread as it ought to be. We will always face the temptation to serve ourselves, abusing power, position and influence. It will be costly to choose the alternative path. We may not get recognised. We may get unfairly overlooked. This is part of the cost, but we can still choose to embrace it willingly and cheerfully. Leadership should never be about us.

Thirdly, this kind of commitment will be **contagious**.

Whilst servant-hearted leadership is not prevalent, it is inherently attractive. Most people yearn to be part of something bigger than themselves and, when you commit to modelling leadership that serves others, those around you will start to follow. Leadership responsibility starts with you. Whenever I coach anyone, I always ask three questions at the end of each session: 1. What might you want to stop? (e.g. an unhelpful behaviour) 2. What might you want to start? (e.g. a new approach) 3. What could you share with someone else? (e.g. a helpful idea or story). STOP, START, SHARE. The third question is particularly important as it focuses our minds on developing others.

Our world desperately needs quality leaders whose interactions with those around them are life-giving and full of hope. This kind of leadership is not focussed on being the leader, but instead focusses on how the leader serves. Imagine a world where every leader is committed to this vision. Will you accept the challenge to positively influence the lives of other people through relationships? I am committed to this cause and I'd love you to join me.

I'm not a leader.
I'm ~~not~~ a leader.
I'm a leader.

And so are you.

ABOUT THE AUTHOR

Mark lives in Guildford, Surrey (UK) and is married to Steph. They have a young family and Mark considers serving them to be the biggest leadership challenge and privilege he has ever undertaken. He has travelled widely, especially across Africa, and loves exploring new places, playing sport, reading and sharing good food with friends.

Having formerly worked as a secondary school teacher, sports coach, construction worker and church pastor, he is now involved in leadership development with C-me Colour Profiling (www.colour-profiling.com), overseeing their work in Education. He also runs his own leadership consultancy (www.leader-full.co.uk), primarily focussed on helping those who are newer to leadership. He is passionate about helping to raise the next generation of leaders.

It is through this wide variety of employments and adventures that Mark has mixed with people from many different walks of life, providing him with an unusually diverse set of experiences. This provides a richness to his understanding and modelling of leadership.

I'd love to connect!
www.leader-full.co.uk
mark@leader-full.co.uk

C me | *colour profiling*

C-me is a quick, powerful and enjoyable tool to help you understand the type of leader you can be.

www.colour-profiling.com

For more information, please contact:
mark@colour-profiling.com

We are delighted to see a book written for those who don't yet see themselves as leaders; as in our experience, that is the majority of people. One of the reasons is a lack of confidence and another is the habit of comparing ourselves to others. All the time we compare ourselves unfavourable to others, we are bound to feel less equipped to lead. As we learn to compare ourselves less, we will hopefully eliminate this limiting habit by understanding how we are unique. That's what C-me does for you - helps you understand your unique identity which gives you great clues as to how you can be yourself and lead with integrity. We wish you well on our journey. We all know the world needs good leadership now more than ever.

Simon Wilsher
C-me Founder

Challenge
Ministries
Swaziland
UK

Raising the next generation of young leaders in Eswatini (Swaziland), Southern Africa.

www.cmswazi.org.uk

For more information, please contact: info@cmswazi.org.uk

Eswatini (Swaziland) is a country blighted by HIV/Aids which has wiped out a generation of parents. There are over 200,000 orphans and vulnerable children. Around half the population are under the age of 21. It is estimated that 70% of the population live in poverty and 50% of young people are unemployed.

Challenge Ministries Swaziland is a charity caring for young people who have been living on the streets and children who are vulnerable and orphaned. We are currently raising over 400 children, many of them in a town called Bulembu which used to be a derelict mining town until CMS took over. Our ethos is to raise these children to become future leaders in their own country. CMS cannot change Swaziland but the young people in our care can become future leaders in politics, education, business, healthcare and the church. *They* are the hope to bring about lasting transformation.

CMS have developed several small enterprises in order to create profits to help fund our childcare work. We have a lodge and hospitality business, a honey factory, a dairy and bakery and most recently have started an essential oils business. These provide employment opportunities for some of our graduates and there is a definite entrepreneurial culture encouraged amongst the children. We want them to learn to help themselves and to help their country by working hard and not relying on handouts.

We are so grateful to Mark Herbert who has run leadership training for our teams in Swaziland and look forward to continuing the partnership as he helps us transform the mindset of not only our staff, but the young people we are nurturing as well. He shares my heart for developing leaders and we benefit immensely from his friendship, expertise and support.

Simon Howard
Chairman of CMS UK

AIMH

Printed in Great Britain
by Amazon